The Fallacy Detective

Thirty-Eight Lessons on How to Recognize Bad Reasoning

by Nathaniel Bluedorn & Hans Bluedorn

illustrated by Rob Corley and Tim Hodge

Workbook Edition • 2015 • Fallacy Detective

The Fallacy Detective
by Nathaniel Bluedorn and Hans Bluedorn

Workbook Print Edition
Library of Congress Control Number: 2013944061
ISBN 978-0-9745315-7-1

Electronic Edition
ISBN 978-0-9745315-6-4

www.fallacydetective.com

Any resemblances in this book
to any person, place, or thing
– living or dead –
just might be on purpose.

Contents

Introduction: What Is a Fallacy?

The Inquiring Mind

Avoiding the Question

Making Assumptions

Statistical Fallacies

Propaganda

Introduction

What Is a Fallacy?

A fallacy is an error in logic – a place where someone has made a mistake in his or her thinking.

> DAD: People just don't use their heads anymore.
> JOHNNY: I don't know about that, Dad. I use my head a lot playing soccer.

Dad and Johnny are talking about two different ways of using heads.

This book is for detectives – fallacy detectives. We've designed this book to be a handy manual for spotting the fallacies you meet in the street, in the newspaper, or in yourself. The goal of this book is to help answer the question: *What is bad reasoning*? We also hope you will find that using your head is fun.

To begin this book, we first show why it is important to stretch and exercise your mind. Then we divide the most common errors in reasoning into three sections: avoiding the question, making assumptions, and statistical fallacies. We explain how you can spot these errors, and we give exercises in fallacy detection. This is followed by a section on the propaganda techniques used by advertisers and politicians. The book ends with The Fallacy Detective Game, where you can have fun with your friends who have been learning logic with you.

When you complete this book, you should
1. know how to spot bad reasoning;
2. put a higher value on good reasoning;
3. know how to avoid fallacies in your own reasoning.

Illustration by Rob Corley.

Thousands of years ago, the Greek philosopher Aristotle began to study and categorize the errors in reasoning he saw. People have found logical fallacies to be the most interesting and useful parts of logic.

The Branches of Logic

We are indebted to James B. Nance for part of this diagram.

As you can see by the circle in this diagram, we do not cover all branches of logic in this book. All of the other branches – including syllogisms, scientific reasoning, argumentation, etc. – are very useful. But we chose informal logical fallacies as the focus of this book.

Lessons

This book is for students aged twelve and up. Adults can use this book too.

We designed the lesson format for both private and classroom use with exercises for many levels of difficulty.

We recommend that you work through this book in a group of two or more people. There is something about multiple people discussing their agreements or disagreements which brings out so much more in the lesson. Each person may want to read the lesson independently, and then talk through it together. However, you can work through this book independently too.

Read each exercise and write your answer in the space available. You can check yourself with the answer key at the back of this book.

If you have trouble understanding a lesson, do the exercises anyway. We designed the exercises to be a teaching tool, so you may catch in the exercises what you did not understand in the lesson. If you miss many of the exercises and you do not know why, you may need to repeat that lesson until you understand it. If you still don't understand something taught in this book, try discussing it with your study group or other people.

We wrote The Fallacy Detective test so teachers can check that their students have paid attention in class. Teachers will find this test at our web site too.

Many teachers suggest that *The Fallacy Detective* is equivalent to approximately one or one-half high school credit in logic or critical thinking.

For more tips on how to use this book in a classroom or to ask us questions, visit our web site www.fallacydetective.com.

The Inquiring Mind

Illustration by Tim Hodge.

Lesson 1

Exercise Your Mind

Our dad and mom always wanted us to grow up with "inquiring minds." We'll introduce you to some of the things that they taught us.

The first problem that we need to address is this: some of us don't like to use our minds – period. Everyone loves to have fun, and some of us even love to work. But we all try to avoid using our minds as much as possible. Hopefully, we can change that.

MOTHER TO HER SON: Dad and I have been talking, and we feel that it isn't good for you to spend so much time playing video games. We feel that, as your parents, we should help you develop your mind...

JOHNNY: Whoa! Cool! Get this! I'm on the seventy-second level, and the Zygon clone monster is going to eat my neutrino grenades...

MOTHER: Could you pause that game for a moment? I'm trying to talk to you about your future.

JOHNNY: What if I want to be a fighter pilot when I grow up. These games help hand-eye coordination.

MOTHER: It's hard to talk to you rationally while...

JOHNNY: Hang on, I'm coming to where I have to jump and shoot at the same...

MOTHER: I've been doing some reading about what video games do to the brain. They've done studies that show that...

JOHNNY: Yikes! He almost got me!

Johnny's mother is trying to get Johnny to engage his mind, but that is exactly what Johnny doesn't want to do. He is having fun, and his game is using as much of his mind as he wants to use.

When a person gets old enough to realize how short his life is, he begins to realize how valuable it would have been if he had learned wisdom early in life.

If there is only one thing you learn from this book, we want to inspire you to exercise your mind – and not let it get fat and flabby.

> FARMER ED: Like I told your father, your aunt Mabel and I haven't made a profit from the farm for years now.
>
> YOUNG NEPHEW BACK FROM AGRICULTURAL COLLEGE: Why don't you try changing some of the ways you do things on your farm?
>
> FARMER ED: I think I'll just stick to what I've got going right now. I don't have the patience to try this new system you're talking about – I'd have to unlearn a lot. Your grandpa always said you can't teach an old dog new tricks. I like your optimism – farming needs people like you – but we're pretty settled here at the farm.

Farmer Ed looks at his nephew's new ideas, and he sees too much hard mental work. He doesn't believe he has the energy to rethink all that he's learned about farming. Farmer Ed might be willing to do the physical work, but it takes mental work to change, and that's what he's afraid of. Thinking is hard work.

The mind is like a muscle. It needs exercise too.

We must discipline our minds the same way an athlete exercises his body. We must exercise our minds so that it does not hurt anymore when we try to use them. This is the first quality of an *inquiring mind*.

Exercises

Read the following examples and decide if the person probably: (a) doesn't want to exercise his mind, (b) has an inquiring mind, or (c) none of the above.

1. SURFER DUDE: Hey, man. Like, I'm never going back to school. These waves are, like, so much more cool. I just can, like, spend my whole life here, man. Like this is the, like, life, man.

   a ▢   *b* ▢   *c* ▢

2. A LITTLE CHILD: I can't put my toys away.... I don't remember where they go.

   a ▢   *b* ▢   *c* ▢

3. TED: Don't make me go into town to pick up groceries. There's a foot of snowfall since last night, and it will be a pain to shovel out the driveway again.

   a ▢   *b* ▢   *c* ▢

4. BRADLEY: My grandpa tried to get me to go to one of those political debates again.
   WESSON: Yeah? You mean between the guys running for mayor? What'd you tell him?
   BRADLEY: He knows I don't go in for that stuff. I don't get what they say. Like, uh, who wants to?

   a ▢   *b* ▢   *c* ▢

5. MARIO: I like reading two different newspapers that report the same event. That way I see the issue from two perspectives.

   a ▢   *b* ▢   *c* ▢

6. BLAINE: Oh, Dad, do I have to? I hate mowing the lawn. I get covered with grass, and my allergies bother me.

   a ☐   b ☐   c ☐

7. KATE: I hate going to the library. I always get caught reading some book and wasting a lot of time. But let's go anyway.

   a ☐   b ☐   c ☐

8. BENNY: If I don't finish reading this book tonight, I'll have to pay a library fine.

   a ☐   b ☐   c ☐

Lesson 2

Love to Listen

This lesson is about listening and the benefits that come from listening.

Illustration by Rob Corley.

At the county fair, Bob joins a circle of guys having a discussion. He catches the words "drives them up" and interjects his thoughts on what's driving up corn prices.

Illustration by Rob Corley.

After several minutes, Bob pauses. The guys try to imagine where he is coming from – they'd been discussing differences between men and women drivers when Bob joined them.

Bob chalks their silence up to shyness and starts explaining little-known factors that affect the price of corn.

Illustration by Rob Corley.

Bob becomes more and more animated – he thinks they don't get his point. Finally, one guy mumbles something about feeding his pigs and strolls away. Everybody else does the same.

What is Bob's problem? Does Bob talk too much? People who know Bob might agree. However, is it possible that his problem is deeper? Can it be that Bob simply does not like to listen – that he enjoys telling people what he thinks more than he enjoys listening to what they have to say?

A person who is humble and who loves to listen may show these characteristics:

1. He is more interested in hearing what other people have to say than in having them listen to him. Humility brings respect for others and for their thoughts.
2. He places a modest value on his own opinions – he admits that other people often have better ideas than he does.
3. He willingly admits when he doesn't know something. If he doesn't understand something, he is open about it.
4. He is willing to question his own position on an issue.

If a person shows these qualities, then he may be someone who loves to listen. And being a person who loves to listen is another ingredient in an *inquiring mind*.

Exercises

Are the people in the following examples (a) showing that they love to listen, (b) showing that they don't love to listen, or (c) neither?

1. GARY: I know I'm right. I don't need to listen to you try to convince me that I'm not right.

   a ☐   *b* ☐   *c* ☐

2. BETTY: Jabber, jabber, jabber. You just talk and talk. Would you give a poor tired body like me some peace and quiet?

   a ☐   *b* ☐   *c* ☐

3. Bryan has been talking for half an hour, nonstop, to his coworker Webster. He now says, "Web, I don't mean to monopolize our discussion. Do you have anything to say? But be quick; I've only got a few seconds."

   a ☐   *b* ☐   *c* ☐

4. JERRY: This music is so loud that it's blowing out my eardrums. Could you turn it down a bit?

   a ☐   *b* ☐   *c* ☐

5. BILL: I'm plugging my ears. I don't want to hear another one of your critical statements about me.

   a ☐   *b* ☐   *c* ☐

6. JIM: I need to stop listening to my friend Nat. I'm beginning to care too much about what he thinks. I'm a real man. I have a right to my own ideas. What do I care? I need to make my own decisions in life.

   a ☐   *b* ☐   *c* ☐

7. PATTY: I just have too many opinions, and I know I jabber on about them too much. My opinions get in the way of learning. I need to just listen more and be more willing to accept other people's ideas.

   a ☐   *b* ☐   *c* ☐

Lesson 3

Opposing Viewpoints

When we are forming an opinion on an issue, it is often a good idea to collect other people's viewpoints on it. The more viewpoints we hear, the better we understand the whole picture.

Illustration by Rob Corley.

Oscar just knew he was right. He didn't need to read about all of those other viewpoints. Oscar knew they were all wrong. The group Oscar was with – called the Flat Earth Society – made sure its members knew why other positions were wrong. The international headquarters published many little booklets which explained everything in simple language. Sometimes Oscar wondered how people could believe that the world was round – and not flat, as his group taught. Oscar figured that most people were just stupid and didn't think about what they believed.

Dr. Weednut, a leading figure in the Flat Earth Society, had an entertaining way of explaining why society has deceived itself into believing that the Earth is round when everyone can see that it is obviously flat. Oscar liked Dr. Weednut the first time he met him. He stimulated Oscar to think, and he made thinking seem so easy. Oscar was glad he had someone whom he could trust to explain everything to him.

Oscar is not honestly evaluating both sides of the issue firsthand. He isn't studying things for himself. He has only listened to one side of the issue – the Flat Earth side. No wonder his side makes sense to him. Any side may seem logical if we only see things from that one point of view.

Many Counselors

When we want to make a decision about something, it is often good to ask for advice from several people. Also, if many people gave us their advice but they all agreed with each other on everything, then we would learn nothing new. That's why we need to listen to advisors who disagree with each other. By hearing a wide range of opinions, we are better able to choose the best advice.

Wilby had a problem. He didn't know which brand of toothpaste to buy. He decided to try this new opposing viewpoints idea he'd been reading about in *The Fallacy Detective*. He decided to go around and ask different people what they thought.

WENDY, A STORE ASSISTANT WHO OFFERED TO HELP: This type with oxy-white pro is guaranteed to make your teeth whiter in twenty-four hours. (Wilby noticed that toothpaste brands with the oxy-white pro sticker were twice the price of other brands.)

PHOEBE, A FRIEND OF WILBY'S: Wilby, I think you'd have such a cute smile if you got rid of some of those blueberry Popsicle stains on your teeth.

JUDD, ANOTHER FRIEND: Toothpaste? What's that? Real men don't brush their teeth.

WILBY'S MOM: Wilby, it really doesn't matter, as long as you don't buy anything that contains fluoride additives. You might come down with a terrible disease in a few years if you use fluoride.

AUSTIN, WILBY'S COWORKER: I only use Hug-A-Tree brand. It's made by an environmentally conscious company from Denmark. They promise they don't test their product on whales.

BOB, WHO WORKS OUT AT THE HEALTH CLUB WITH WILBY: I heard on a talk show that if you chew organic mint leaves, then your breath will smell good without having to brush your teeth.

Wilby concluded that he was worrying too much over nothing. He decided to keep using the brand of toothpaste he'd always used. It seemed to do the job. But now he understood more about how different people make their decisions.

We gain two benefits from looking at opposing viewpoints:

1. We can change our views if we are wrong. We would never have this opportunity if we listened only to things with which we agreed.
2. We can better help others. When we study a viewpoint which is wrong, we still learn many things. It helps us to understand how to defend our own views, and it helps us to communicate our views to others.

No one has the time to evaluate every viewpoint on every issue, but we can try to learn more about alternative views. This is another part of having an *inquiring mind*.

Exercises

In the list of issues below, try to think of at least two sides to each issue. Some of these are well-known opposing viewpoints. If you find a different pair of opposing viewpoints than we do in the answer key, that is all right. We have done the first one for you.

1. The Civil War

   Example: the view of the Union and the view of the Confederacy

2. The reasons for the American Revolution

3. Taxes

4. The existence of God

5. Baseball teams

6. Breeds of dogs

7. Gun control

8. The origin of the universe and of life

9. Slavery in America before 1860

10. Logic

11. Should little boys take baths?

12. The color pink

Avoiding the Question

Lesson 4

Red Herring Fallacy

Consider the following conversation:

JENNY: Girls are much smarter than boys.

BERT: Oh yeah. How do you know that?

JENNY: Because they just are.

BERT: But how do you know it?

JENNY: There are lots of girls who have done lots of smart things. Our neighbor Mrs. Jones is pretty smart; Joan of Arc saved the French from the English; and Madame Curie invented the light bulb.

BERT: But how do you know they are smarter than boys?

JENNY: Because there are many girls who have high IQs. That makes them smart.

BERT: You still haven't answered the question. Why are girls smarter than boys?

JENNY: Well, I'm smart and you're dumb. That proves it.

It should be clear that Jenny isn't really answering the question. She is saying things that sound like they answer the question, but they don't. She is trying to prove that girls are smarter than boys, but she is only showing that some girls are smart and says nothing about how smart boys are.

It isn't that she is saying things that aren't true (except for the part about Madame Curie). But she isn't answering the real question of "why are girls smarter than boys?" If she were to really answer the question, she could say something like:

JENNY: Girls are smarter than boys because it has been proven that the average IQ of a girl is higher than the average IQ of a boy.

You see, when we argue, it can be difficult to stay on the topic – to answer the question we are arguing. It is easy to introduce something irrelevant into the argument. Also, it can be even more difficult to notice when somebody else is straying from the topic and introducing something irrelevant into the argument.

Whenever we introduce something irrelevant into an argument, we are *avoiding the question*.

Red Herring

When someone is avoiding the question and asserting something irrelevant, we say they are introducing a *red herring* into the argument. A red herring is a dead fish – a dead fish that has started to become "ripe" and smelly. Dog trainers used red herrings to train their tracking dogs. They would lay out a scent trail of a raccoon (or whatever they wanted the dog to learn to track) and let the trail become old, then they would drag the red herring (which by this time was very "ripe" and smelly) across the trail and off in a different direction. Then they would train the dog to stay on the raccoon's scent trail and ignore the red herring's scent trail. So, a red herring is a distracting scent trail. In our context, a red herring is an irrelevant topic which distracts us from the real question.

A *red herring* introduces an irrelevant point into an argument. Someone may think (or may want us to think) it proves his side, but it really doesn't.

I am sure this has happened to you before: you are talking with somebody about something you disagree on, and after a while you realize that you aren't discussing the thing you started out discussing. This is because somewhere in the argument, somebody introduced a red herring, and you have been arguing about the red herring ever since.

JENNY: I think boys should always open doors for girls.
BERT: Why?
JENNY: Because that is the gentlemanly thing to do.

BERT: Why is that the gentlemanly thing to do?

JENNY: Because it is very helpful for the girls.

BERT: But wouldn't it also be a helpful thing for boys if all the girls opened the doors for them? Why don't all the girls open the doors for boys?

JENNY: Because that isn't right. This afternoon, when we were coming out of the grocery store, I had several bags in my hands, and I had to put them all down to open the door just because you were too rude to help me.

BERT: I couldn't help you open the door because I was out in the parking lot waiting in the car.

JENNY: See what I mean? You were too inconsiderate to think that I might need some help when I came out of the grocery store. I think that was very ungentlemanly.

BERT: I didn't know that you were going to buy so many groceries; otherwise I would have.

JENNY: You should have thought of that.

Do you notice that Bert and Jenny aren't arguing anymore about whether boys should open doors for girls? Now, they are arguing about whether Bert should have opened the door for Jenny that afternoon. This is because Jenny introduced a red herring into the argument, and Bert didn't notice. Bert should have said something like:

BERT: Maybe I should have opened the door for you today, but how does that show that boys should always open doors for girls?

To properly answer the question, Jenny could have said:

JENNY: Because girls have smaller hands than boys, so they can't turn door-knobs as easily.

While there are some better arguments for why boys should open doors for girls, this one at least addresses the topic.

Calvin is introducing some red herrings here.
What he says has nothing to do with whether his dad should retrieve the ball.

Not a Red Herring

When somebody says "I don't know" and doesn't answer the question, he is not introducing a red herring. He is still addressing the topic – he just doesn't have an answer.

> SON: What is the square root of 234.09667?
> FATHER: I don't know. Why don't you go figure it out on a calculator?

The father here is addressing his son's question. He just doesn't know the answer.

Exercises

In the following examples, is the speaker addressing the question and staying on topic? If he isn't and he is introducing something irrelevant, shout "RED HERRING!" at the top of your lungs.

1. SON: Why can't I go see the movie *The Day of the Spatulas* with my friends?

DAD: Because it's a scary movie, and you shouldn't see scary movies when you are this young.

RED HERRING! ☐   not red herring ☐

2. SON: Why can't I go see *The Day of the Spatulas* with my friends?
   DAD: Because January 1 falls on a Wednesday this year.

   RED HERRING! ☐   not red herring ☐

3. SON: Why can't I go see *The Day of the Spatulas* with my friends?
   FRIEND: Because you don't have enough money for the ticket.

   RED HERRING! ☐   not red herring ☐

4. SON: Why can't I go see *The Day of the Spatulas* with my friends?
   DAD: Isn't there some other kind of movie you could go to see instead?

   RED HERRING! ☐   not red herring ☐

5. SON: Dad, can I go see *The Day of the Spatulas* with my friends?
   DAD: Why don't you go ask your mother?

   RED HERRING! ☐   not red herring ☐

6. SON: Dad, can I go see *The Day of the Spatulas* with my friends?
   DAD: No.

   RED HERRING! ☐   not red herring ☐

7. SON: Dad, can I go see *The Day of the Spatulas* with my friends?
    DAD: I don't know. What is *The Day of the Spatulas*? Is it about pancakes?

    RED HERRING!   *not red herring*

8. SON: Dad, why did you go to see the movie *The Day of the Spatulas* when you said I couldn't?
    DAD: It was a really good movie. I'll take you to see it next week.

    RED HERRING!   *not red herring*

Lesson 5

Recognizing Red Herrings

When someone introduces a red herring, he may be saying something which is true although irrelevant.

"Sparkledent is great for reducing cavities. Dentists say cavities are the number one dental problem in America."

This advertisement is saying something which is true: cavities are a big problem. However, it says nothing about how Sparkledent will reduce cavities. If the ad said something like "Sparkledent is recommended by dentists everywhere as the number one cavity-reducing toothpaste, so you should use it," then it would be addressing the issue. Instead, it introduces a red herring.

Illustration by Rob Corley.

Porcupines make good pets.
Studies show owning a pet makes children happy!

Red herrings are often good arguments. The only problem is they don't prove the point being argued – they prove something else.

SON: Spinach can't be good for me – it tastes terrible.

MOM: It may taste terrible, but you still have to show me it isn't good for you.

It is often difficult to recognize when somebody is introducing a red herring. Here is an example which is a little harder to recognize. A tract from XYZ Ministries titled *Ten Reasons to Believe in Life After Death* gives the following as reason number one:

"The Injustices of Life: it would be difficult to believe that life is good if we knew there was nothing beyond the grave to compensate for problems of inequality and unfairness. While some people seem destined for happiness, others are born into terrible relationships and circumstances."

If we summarized this, we might say "We should believe in life after death because it would be unfair if there wasn't life after death." The author does makes a case that life can feel unfair and an afterlife might make it seem less unfair. However, his argument does not show us that there *is* an afterlife. Therefore, this argument does not show us that we should believe in an afterlife – his argument is irrelevant. The only reason for anybody to believe in an afterlife (or anything else for that matter) is if there really is one – not because believing in it makes us feel good.

Exercises

In the following examples, answer these questions: (1) What is the question that is being argued? (2) Is the speaker addressing the question and staying on topic? If he isn't, and he is introducing something irrelevant, scream "RED

HERRING" at the top of your lungs.

1. "Grizzly bears can't be dangerous to humans – they look so cute."

RED HERRING! ☐   *not red herring* ☐

2. "Why should I study math? I don't want to be a math teacher."

RED HERRING! ☐   *not red herring* ☐

3. "People should make an effort to read a book a month because reading books will build their minds and their vocabulary. Building the mind and vocabulary is a good thing."

RED HERRING! ☐   *not red herring* ☐

4. "I think that the government should raise taxes. It doesn't have enough money to spend on the programs that the American people need. The only way for the government to get enough money is to raise taxes."

RED HERRING! ☐   *not red herring* ☐

5. "I think the government should lower taxes. The government is spending too much money on welfare programs. The people on welfare are ruining our economy by making us give our hard-earned money to them, when most of them could go out and get a job and earn it themselves. When people are on welfare, it lowers productivity and hurts the economy."

RED HERRING! ☐   *not red herring* ☐

6. TEN REASONS TO BELIEVE IN LIFE AFTER DEATH, REASON NUMBER TEN – PRACTICAL EFFECTS: Belief in life after death is a source of personal security, optimism, and spiritual betterment. Nothing offers more courage than the confidence that there is a better life for those who use the present to prepare for eternity.

RED HERRING! ☐   *not red herring* ☐

7. PRESIDENTIAL CANDIDATE WHEN ASKED WHETHER HE'D NAME A RUNNING MATE WHO WAS OPPOSED TO ABORTION: It would be incredibly presumptive for someone who has yet to earn his party's nomination to be picking a vice president. However, the main criterion I would use in choosing a running mate would be whether the person was capable of being president.

RED HERRING! ☐   *not red herring* ☐

8. PRESIDENTIAL CANDIDATE WHEN ASKED WHETHER HE EVER USED DRUGS: No, I have never touched the stuff in my life.

RED HERRING!   *not red herring*

9. PRESIDENTIAL CANDIDATE WHEN ASKED WHETHER HE EVER CHEATED ON A TEST IN SCHOOL: I don't think that is any of your business. I don't think I have to answer questions like that, so I am not going to say.

RED HERRING!   *not red herring*

10. "Now, some in Congress believe the national government has no business helping communities improve their schools....But I think strengthening education is a national priority." – Bill Clinton

RED HERRING!   *not red herring*

11. "How can deforestation be bad when there are many uses for the wood?"

RED HERRING!   *not red herring*

Lesson 6

Special Pleading

We've learned how people use red herrings to avoid a question. Now we'll look at some methods they use to do this. One method involves double standards. A double standard treats people or ideas unfairly.

> ASHER: Why are you eating that? I thought we were on a diet and we weren't going to snack between meals.
>
> IMOGEN: It's only cookie dough. It's not even cooked. It doesn't really count as snacking if it isn't cooked yet.

Imogen and Asher have decided to not snack between meals, but Imogen is making an exception with cookie dough because it isn't cooked yet.

When someone uses a double standard or argues for an unjustified exception, he is committing the fallacy of *special pleading*.

The special pleading fallacy is a type of red herring. When someone introduces an unjustified exception to an argument, he is avoiding the issue. He is saying something like, "Most people shouldn't rob banks, but I'm an exception. I need the money!"

> "I know I need to control my anger. But, Officer, this time my sister was nagging me so much and the only thing I could do was lock her in the closet."

When someone is emotionally involved in an issue, he may want to make his actions an exception to the rule. This boy is mad at his sister, and he thinks her nagging gives him an excuse to do something very wrong.

To recognize special pleading, we need to step back and ask ourselves:

Why is this exception relevant? Is this distracting us from the issue involved? Special pleading fallacies often involve fairness.

> NEWSPAPER ARTICLE: Arkansas law requires that everyone follow the speed limit and obey traffic lights. But Hick County officials say that they discourage police officers from giving tickets to fellow officers and their families. "Police officers have the right to stop anyone, but it's only reasonable that they show professional courtesy to their fellow officers," said Sheriff Marty Boone. "It's one of the perks."

There are times when a police officer needs to break the speed limit or run a red light to reach an accident quickly or catch a criminal. But when this is not the case, this may be special pleading.

Illustration by Tim Hodge.

We can't make ourselves an exception to the law.

Exercises

Which of the following examples are red herring, special pleading, or neither?

1. JENNY: What's that?
   BERT: An oud. It's a fretless stringed instrument from the Middle East.

JENNY: Can you play it?

BERT: Professional oud players can make lots of money.

red herring		special pleading		neither	

2. GRANDMA: I'm not gambling! This is bingo, not poker. It's different. We're not using a deck of cards.

red herring		special pleading		neither	

3. DOG BREEDER: My puppies cost $1,200 each.

CUSTOMER: Could you reduce the price of your puppies to $500 for me? I only want to find a furry friend to love me.

red herring		special pleading		neither	

4. CLETUS: May the peace of the universe be in your consciousness in these times of strife.

DOMBREZEL: Yes, and may these times of strife bring the center of the galaxy into a fuller understanding of its own existence.

red herring		special pleading		neither	

5. "Can I be next in the bathroom? I have to go bad."

red herring		special pleading		neither	

6. "Can I be next in the bathroom? I have to curl my hair, but you're just going to take a shower."

red herring		special pleading		neither	

7. RICH WOMAN TO HER MAID: I know you think I shouldn't spend millions on my antique hat collection and should give this money to the poor instead. But being rich is hard. It's just something you'll never understand.

red herring		special pleading		neither	

8. MISS: I don't want to get engaged.
MR.: Things were going so well!
MISS: I heard your dad was in prison when you were born. I don't want to be married to someone whose family was into illegal activities.

red herring		special pleading		neither	

9. GRANDSON: Grandma, can I have more money for my birthday? You gave $20 to Johnny. I'm two years older. You should give me $22.

red herring		special pleading		neither	

10. SISTER: You're tracking mud in the house! Why do you think you're always an exception to the rule about...
BROTHER: Quick! Where's the phone! I have to call 911! A skydiver fell in our tree, and I think he's hurt!

red herring		special pleading		neither	

11. SISTER: You're tracking mud in the house again! Why do you think you're an exception...
BROTHER: I won't do it next time. But this time I forgot my keys and I'm in a hurry.

red herring		special pleading		neither	

Lesson 7

Ad Hominem Attack

Sometimes people attack the person making an argument instead of the argument itself. Let us look at an exchange that we hope never took place:

G. WASHINGTON: I disagree with my distinguished opponent regarding his views on public housing for minorities. I think that it would be wrong for us to force the taxpayers to fund such an enterprise.

T. JEFFERSON: I must insist that my opponent is mistaken in his beliefs, and the public should, in fact, disregard them. My reason is that he has been in the military most of his life, and therefore he cannot have compassion for the feelings and needs of minorities.

G. WASHINGTON: I must again disagree. My opinion is not influenced by my rank in life and my position in the military. My opponent, however, is not so clean from bias. His desire for public funding for housing for minorities stems from an unbalanced pity for them and his insane desire to further their cause. His opinion cannot be trusted.

T. JEFFERSON: Whoa. We want to talk about biases, do we? What about your bigoted hatred for the Indians? If that doesn't influence your beliefs about minorities, then I don't know what would.

G. WASHINGTON: My feelings about the Indians have nothing to do with this. But as long as we are insinuating things, I'm just wondering what you did on all of those trips to France. Nobody seems to know.

T. JEFFERSON: What are *you* doing now? Attacking my character? Have I ever said anything about that cherry tree?

Here, neither debater is conducting himself in a distinguished way. Neither is addressing his opponent's arguments. Instead, each is attacking his opponent's person. This is common in debates – especially political debates. If one debater can discredit his opponent's character or motives, then the public will often think badly of his opponent's argument as well.

Illustration by Rob Corley.

Can a shrimp like this run our great country?

An *ad hominem* attack is attacking an opponent's character or his motives for believing something instead of disproving his argument.

"*Ad hominem*" is Latin for "to the man."

> JENNY: My uncle says that all murderers should be put to death because then nobody would want to murder anybody anymore.
> SYLVIA: Wasn't your uncle in jail once? I don't think that we can trust the opinion of someone who was once a criminal.

This is not the right way to argue. Someone may have character flaws, but his argument can still be valid.

Charles Darwin lived in the 1800s and developed the theory of evolution. At the time, many people thought his idea that humans descended from apes was ridiculous. However, Darwin also studied earthworms. He did experiments to show that earthworms helped the soil and weren't pests like most people thought at the time. Someone from Darwin's time might have said this about him:

> We shouldn't believe Darwin when he says earthworms are good. He also believes that monkeys can turn into men!

This would be an irrelevant argument. This argument attacks Darwin's other theories, not his reasons for saying that earthworms are good. This person should examine Darwin's reasons for saying that earthworms are good, and he can ignore other theories he may disagree with.

Ad hominem also occurs when somebody accuses his opponent of having bad motives.

> JENNY: My uncle says that Robert E. Lee was a good, honest man.
>
> SYLVIA: Doesn't your uncle come from Alabama? That's in the South. I don't think we need to give much weight to your uncle's arguments if he is from the South. He's obviously biased.

Jenny's uncle may be biased, but Sylvia shouldn't totally disregard his opinion because of that. A person's character or motives may influence his arguments, but these things don't necessarily have any bearing on the strength of his arguments.

Not Ad Hominem

It is not an *ad hominem* when someone only questions whether someone else is telling the truth.

> "I don't think we can trust Mr. Smith when he says that he was nowhere near the scene of the crime. He has been known to lie on many occasions, and he certainly has a motive for not telling the truth here."

The speaker here is not discrediting Mr. Smith's *opinion* by saying he has a bad character. He is discrediting Mr. Smith's ability *to state the facts* – he can't be trusted to tell the truth.

Exercises

What form of bad reasoning, if any, do you find in the following examples? If there is no bad reasoning, write "none."

1. "Senator Ribbet is a liar. You shouldn't listen to his opinion on anything."

2. "Senator Ribbet is a liar. You can't believe him when he tells you something."

3. "I know everybody thinks Einstein's theory of relativity is correct, but I can't accept it. Einstein didn't comb his hair."

4. "We all know Senator Ribbet's view on the war. But what about that incident where he got drunk, crashed his car, and ended up killing somebody? In light of that, how can we listen to his views?"

5. "I never met a man I didn't like."

6. "Mr. Jones has some good-sounding ideas. His idea of reducing costs while increasing output sounds promising. However, did you know that Mr. Jones was an alcoholic before he came to work with us?"

7. MOM: Did you take out the trash, Bert?
    BERT: Why are you always suspecting me of things?

8. MRS. A: I'm going through a logic book with my kids. It's called *The Fallacy Detective*. I really like it.
    MRS. B: Aw, the authors of that book are just a couple of homeschoolers. What do they know about logic?

9. DISTINGUISHED SENATOR A: I am in favor of the federal government building a dam over the Watchichokiehatchie River. I think it would help agriculture in the region, which would benefit this country's economy greatly.
    DISTINGUISHED SENATOR B: That is fine for you to say. The Watchichokiehatchie River is located in your state, and if this bill goes through and the dam is built, then you will probably be reelected next term.

10. BERT: I heard that Joseph Stalin was an evil, cruel man who stopped at nothing to gain power over Europe during WWII.
    JENNY: What! Without the help of Stalin, we couldn't have beaten the Germans.

11. "My cousin says he is getting a real race car for his birthday. He says it can go 298 miles per hour. I don't believe him. He lies about everything."

12. WAR HISTORIAN: During World War II, the Nazis used torture, such as beating and electric shocks, to get members of the French Resistance to

divulge how they planned to attack the Germans.

U.S. ARMY SERGEANT: But wouldn't you agree that we need to use "extreme interrogation techniques" to get terrorists to tell us their plans? Otherwise, they might kill thousands of people, like in New York on September 11.

13. JENNY: The American Revolution was one of the highest points in American history. During that time period, great strides were taken in the development of a just government.

CLYDE: Naw, it wasn't. I heard George Washington owned slaves.

Lesson 8

Genetic Fallacy

The genetic fallacy is another personal attack fallacy. It is called "genetic" because it addresses the genesis, or beginning, of something. The genetic fallacy is different from *ad hominem* because it does not attack the person making the argument. It attacks the place where the argument came from.

Illustration by Tim Hodge.

Ew! Did you know flip-flops were invented by hippies?

The *genetic fallacy* is condemning an argument because of where it began, how it began, or who began it.

JENNY: I think capital punishment is wrong. We should never put people to death.

CLYDE: Ah. The only reason why you disagree with capital punishment is because you were abused as a child and have never gotten over it.

It is very difficult to argue with somebody when he uses this fallacy. No matter what you say, he will just claim you are saying it because of your difficult past, and therefore, everybody can ignore what you say.

It seems that people think that if an idea came out of the Russian Revolution or was first proposed by a criminal, then it has to be bad. The idea may be bad, but it is not *necessarily* bad because of the source. If an argument was made up by a bad person or came out of a bad historical event, it doesn't mean the argument is bad itself.

"[We need to question whether the person who won the electoral college vote – but didn't get the popular vote – should become president, because]… the electoral college was invented largely as a scheme to allow southern states to count slaves as three-fifths human, ensuring their domination of national elections for the first decades of the Republic." – Jesse Jackson

The electoral college (which is the system the Constitution laid out for choosing the president) may have been created by people with bad motives, but that doesn't necessarily make the electoral college bad *now*. Many factors may have changed since then.

BERT: Mr. Gritchus, why do you always wear suspenders and never a belt?

MR. GRITCHUS: Because belts were developed in the military centuries ago and were used by soldiers. Since the military is evil, and belts came from the military, I can't wear a belt.

Even if belts did come out of the military – which Mr. Gritchus thinks is evil – that fact doesn't mean that if Mr. Gritchus wears one, then he is *in* the military and participating in their evil. He may still wear them for good reasons – like holding up his pants.

Exercises

What form of bad reasoning, if any, do you find in the following examples? If there is no bad reasoning, write "none."

1. "You can tell a lot about a fellow's character by his way of eating jelly beans." – Ronald Reagan

2. "Good grief! You're thirty-five years old and you still believe in Santa Claus? You only believe that because you fell down a well when you were three and haven't recovered since."

3. "You disagree with the idea of women in the military just because of your conservative upbringing."

4. BERT: This encyclopedia says Columbus discovered America in 1492.
   JENNY: The one I have here says he discovered America in 1924. How many volumes are in your encyclopedia?
   BERT: Four.
   JENNY: Well, that proves it. Mine has eighteen. Mine must be right.

5. "Taking drugs can't be bad. There are lots of people who enjoy it."

6. "Our earliest human ancestors had fears. They had fears of having accidents, of becoming sick and dying, and of being harmed by rival tribes.

As a result, certain persons within a tribe would claim they had powers to protect others from these dangers. They had certain spells and incantations which they said would protect people from harm. This belief, over the course of history, developed into the belief in gods. I see no reason to believe there is a God, since this belief only came from our desires to stop worrying."

7. "I think I heard that the famous author O. Henry was in prison once. I don't think I'm going to read any more of his books."

8. "The fashions in London come straight from Paris, and the fashions in Paris come straight from Hades."

9. "Senator A has given us reasons for increasing the pay for military personnel. But we all know that Senator A has three sons who are in the military, so his family would benefit greatly if their pay was increased."

Lesson 9

Tu Quoque

Tu quoque is Latin for "you too."

Tu quoque is dismissing someone's viewpoint on an issue because he himself is inconsistent in that very thing.

> FRED: I wouldn't smoke cigarettes if I were you. It is a bad habit, and it will bring you all kinds of problems.
>
> JAKE: Don't tell me not to smoke. You do it too.

Jake's comment is irrelevant to Fred's concerns – smoking is still bad for Jake. Fred might have some very good reasons for telling Jake not to smoke cigarettes. He may have begun smoking when he was young, and now he can't stop. Fred may not want to see Jake ruin his life like Fred did.

People who commit this fallacy often have guilty consciences, and it makes them feel better somehow when they shift their guilt onto someone else.

> "I don't see what is wrong with Spanish bullfighting. I enjoy watching it myself. I know a lot of people say it is cruel and unmercifully violent. But look at the kinds of sports you Americans enjoy: boxing – where two people beat each other up until one falls down, and football – where two teams tackle each other and a whole team piles up on one man. And what about your violent movies? You watch movies where people are killed and dismembered right before your very eyes."

This man doesn't address the point: is Spanish bullfighting cruel? He hopes to shift attention onto everybody else's actions.

This fallacy also happens when somebody claims that two wrongs make a right.

"Oh, Vito, what've I done to make you to treat me so disrespectfully? You murdered my brother Frankie – I had no choice but to have that bomb delivered to your home. Only now can I be avenged."

The fact that somebody did something wrong to you doesn't mean you have a right to do the same back to them.

Illustration by Rob Corley.

Exercises

What form of bad reasoning, if any, do you find in the following examples? If there is no bad reasoning, write "none."

1. "I don't see what right you have to question where I get my money for my campaigns. Wasn't it you, four years ago, who became entangled in a big scandal where twenty-three congressmen were caught laundering money through the congressional post office?"

2. "While [Jesse] Jackson emphasized from the start that the dispute [over whether to allow several black youths back in school, after they had caused a fight] was about 'fairness' and not race, some of the protesters Sunday…noted that all of the board members who voted to expel the students were white and the only dissenting vote was from a black member."

3. "That company's products can't possibly be good. It was started by a narcissistic creep."

4. "My opponent cannot be trusted when he says he has had no illegal contributions to his campaign. Last term, he was caught lying on several occasions."

5. In response to someone's comment that the military is overcommitted and underresourced and worse off today than it was eight years ago, Senator Joseph Lieberman said, "Most importantly, I want to assure the American people the American military is the best-trained, best-equipped, most powerful force in the world and that Al Gore and I will do whatever it takes to keep them that way."

6. "Only those who are chronically obese would oppose dietary restrictions."

7. "O. J. Simpson couldn't have murdered his wife. He's in the Pro Football Hall of Fame. He's famous!"

8. JENNY: I think all wars are evil. They are just about killing, and we shouldn't get involved with them.
BERT: Do you think war is wrong even if our country is being invaded?
JENNY: That's impossible. Our country will never be invaded. We are friends with Canada, Mexico would never think of it, and nobody could go all the way across the ocean.
BERT: Ah, but you're wrong. Our country was invaded in 1941 when Pearl Harbor was attacked.
JENNY: But Pearl Harbor was a naval base at that time and not in a state.

9. "I hear all these environmentalists talking about how we should save the environment and all that. It seems kind of ridiculous to me. These same people go to the grocery store and put their groceries in plastic bags, they have houses made out of wood, and they drive gas-guzzling cars. I think they're ridiculous."

10. "I think Joseph Stalin was a dirty rotten scoundrel. I heard that he murdered his wife. It wouldn't surprise me from what other things I have heard about him."

Lesson 10

Faulty Appeal to Authority

When we aren't knowledgeable on a certain subject, the wise thing is to ask an authority – somebody who is knowledgeable on the subject.

> YOU: My car won't run. What's wrong with it?
>
> MECHANIC: Hmmmm.... It looks like the timing chain is broken, the camshaft is warped, and the U-joints are shot. That will have to be fixed before it will run.

You do what the mechanic says because he knows more about cars than you do. The mechanic is the authority, and you trust him.

We all do this every day without thinking about it. When we want to know how high Mount McKinley is, we don't take a yardstick and climb up 20,320 feet to find out. We look it up in a book. We trust that book because the authors have been to Mount McKinley and we haven't. They are authorities on the subject. An *authority* is someone who has special knowledge on a particular subject.

> PROSECUTING ATTORNEY: Mrs. Jones, were you there when your husband was murdered?
>
> MRS. JONES: Yes.
>
> PROSECUTING ATTORNEY: And who was the murderer?
>
> MRS. JONES: That man right there!

Mrs. Jones is an authority on the subject of what happened at the murder scene because she was there.

We are *appealing to an authority* when we claim something is true because an authority said it was true. This can be good if we do it in the right way. However, if the person we are appealing to is not actually an authority in the area we are discussing, our appeal is faulty.

> "My car mechanic says the best way to fix computer problems is to just give the computer a good, sharp kick. He says it should always work."

Your car mechanic may be knowledgeable when working with cars, but it is not likely he has any special knowledge about computers. We should not appeal to him as an authority on computers.

A *faulty appeal to authority* is an appeal to someone who has no special knowledge in the area being discussed.

Unfortunately, some people use an appeal to authority just to overawe someone.

> BERT: I've been a vegetarian all of my life, and I think it has made me healthier than most people.
>
> CLYDE: You think so, huh? I was just reading in a magazine where they interviewed the man who has the highest IQ in the world. This man said he didn't think being a vegetarian made you healthy. He said he didn't think vegetarians received enough fats, so they become weak and fall over a lot. Do you still think being vegetarian is a good idea?
>
> BERT: That sounds bad … especially if that man is the smartest person in the world. He must know plenty. Maybe being vegetarian doesn't help me as much as I thought.

Clyde is using a faulty appeal to authority against Bert. Bert is being overawed by the intelligence of the man with the highest IQ in the world. If Bert thought about it a little more, he would realize that the smartest man in the world may be good at logic problems, and he may be able to beat anybody at Scrabble or chess, but that doesn't mean he knows anything about the effects of not eating meat on the human body.

When someone uses an appeal to authority as a way to overawe us and make us reluctant to challenge that authority's viewpoint, he is committing a *faulty appeal to authority*.

Movie stars are often used in faulty appeals to authority.

"If Paul Newman thinks organic foods are more nutritious than chemically saturated foods, shouldn't you too?"

We have no reason to think Paul Newman is an authority on nutrition. If someone is a respected authority on one subject – such as acting – we tend to think he will also be an authority in other areas – like nutrition. Nobody wants to contradict a movie star, especially if he's good-looking.

When the topic under discussion is controversial among respected authorities, appealing simply to the opinion of a single authority is a *faulty appeal to authority*.

If many accepted authorities disagree on a particular subject, we can't say *our* favorite authority is the correct one. There may be many other equally respected authorities who disagree.

BERT: I've been homeschooled all of my life, and I think it has helped me a lot.

CLYDE: Not according to the president of the National Schooling Association. He says homeschooling stunts a child's social, moral, and academic development and turns a kid into a geeky nerd. You must believe the president of the National Schooling Association. He is a respected authority on the subject of education.

BERT: That's funny; the chairman of the National *Homeschooling* Association says homeschooling produces people who are intelligent, socially adaptable, and bring great benefits to society. He also says that public school students often turn into social troublemakers. You must believe the chairman of the National Homeschooling Association. He is a very respected authority on education.

Homeschooling is a controversial topic among educators of all types. Neither Clyde nor Bert can say homeschooling is good or bad just because a particular authority on education said so. They need to prove their sides in other ways, such as statistical evidence.

Illustration by Rob Corley.

A Montana timberman is usually not an authority
on fixing computer problems.

Exercises

A. Which of the following appeals to authority are good and which ones are faulty?

1. PROSECUTING ATTORNEY: In relation to the scene of the crime, where were you at the time of the murder?
    WITNESS: I was two blocks away, mowing my lawn.
    PROSECUTING ATTORNEY: And what did you see?
    WITNESS: I heard what sounded like a gunshot, so I looked up and I saw the defendant running away from where the murder was committed. I figured he must have murdered someone, so I tackled him and called the cops.

PROSECUTING ATTORNEY: See, there you have it, straight from a man who was there at the scene of the crime. He says this man is guilty.

good appeal to authority ☐

faulty appeal to authority ☐

2. DEFENSE ATTORNEY: What is your relationship to my client?
WITNESS: I cut his hair about once a month when he comes in to my barber shop.
DEFENSE ATTORNEY: And do you think this man is capable of murder?
WITNESS: No, he seemed like a mild-mannered guy to me.
DEFENSE ATTORNEY: There you have it, straight from someone who knows him. My client is not capable of committing this heinous crime.

good appeal to authority ☐

faulty appeal to authority ☐

3. DEFENSE ATTORNEY: What is your relationship to my client?
WITNESS: I am his wife.
DEFENSE ATTORNEY: Would you consider him capable of murder?
WITNESS: He couldn't squash a mosquito if it was biting him; he's that mild-mannered.
DEFENSE ATTORNEY: There you have it. This man's wife says he is not capable of murder.

good appeal to authority ☐

faulty appeal to authority ☐

4. YOU: I'm having trouble playing my violin. Do you have any suggestions?
MECHANIC: Maybe if you blow in the other end instead?

good appeal to authority ☐

faulty appeal to authority ☐

5. YOU: I'm having trouble playing my violin. Do you have any suggestions?
    VIOLIN TEACHER: Hmmmm.... I can see why you are having trouble.
    That isn't a violin. It's a bassoon.

    good appeal to ☐   *faulty appeal to* ☐
    authority   *authority*

6. "My uncle says you shouldn't spank kids when they are bad. He says it's
    ineffective."

    good appeal to ☐   *faulty appeal to* ☐
    authority   *authority*

7. "I'm not ever going to buy a Ford. My mechanic says they break down
    easily. He says all the other mechanics agree with him."

    good appeal to ☐   *faulty appeal to* ☐
    authority   *authority*

8. DOCTOR: Take two pills, and call me in the morning.
    PATIENT: Why?
    DOCTOR: Because I think it will be good for you.

    good appeal to ☐   *faulty appeal to* ☐
    authority   *authority*

B. What form of bad reasoning, if any, do you find in the following examples?
If there is no bad reasoning, write "none."

9. "Have your teeth straightened at Acme Braces. If you want to know how
    good people look after we're done with them, just ask Emma Watson."

    _____

10. JUDGE: Mr. Jones, can you explain to me why you broke all your neigh-
    bor's windows?
    ACCUSED: They were playing loud 70s music. I hate 70s music.
    JUDGE: Didn't you know it's wrong to break your neighbor's windows?

ACCUSED: I heard obnoxious music, so I took action. Playing loud music in town is against the law, isn't it?

11. JUDGE: Why were you playing 70s music so loud? Don't you know we have a city ordinance against loud music?
NEIGHBOR: That rule shouldn't apply. Everyone should enjoy 70s because it is part of our city's heritage.

12. "I think scientists are wrong. There is no such thing as global warming. I just finished talking to my boss, and he thought the idea was ridiculous."

13. "This book called *The Fallacy Detective* says it is a fallacy to appeal to somebody who isn't an authority on any subject. This book must be right because the authors sure know plenty about logical thinking."

14. "I don't think we need to bother listening to your views on this. We all know you are just one of those hyper-liberals."

15. ZACK: Look at this movie *It Happened Before Brunch*. Let's check this one out.
JENNY: No, it looks weird. The cover has a picture of somebody's big toe.
ZACK: No, it has to be good. My friend Cletus recommended it. Cletus has a very high IQ. He wouldn't recommend a movie that was weird.

Lesson 11

Appeal to the People

PERSON CALLING PHONE COMPANY: I heard that you are now charging us for local calls. I am calling to complain. You have no right to charge us for that – you are making enough money as it is. You are the only phone company around here, so you think you can get away with highway robbery.

PHONE COMPANY: I hear what you are saying and appreciate your openness on these issues.

PERSON: I don't want you to appreciate anything. I don't want to pay for local calls.

PHONE COMPANY: You see, when we were discussing this issue, it came to our attention that it is now common in this country to pay for local calls. In fact, the people over in the next state are paying for them now.

PERSON: So?

PHONE COMPANY: Did you know that the people in most European countries have been paying for local calls for years?

PERSON: So?

PHONE COMPANY: It's funny that you have been the only person to call and complain about this new policy. Everybody else seems to be taking it just fine.

PERSON: So?

PHONE COMPANY: Thank you for your input… Click…

The phone company is not addressing the caller's arguments. The phone company is bringing up irrelevant topics. It is irrelevant that people in the United States commonly pay for local calls. It is irrelevant that Europe has been paying for them. And it is just as irrelevant that the caller is the only person to complain about the new policy. The phone company is avoiding the question. The phone company is committing the fallacy of *appeal to the people*.

64

When we claim that our viewpoint is correct because many other people agree with it, we are committing the *appeal to the people* fallacy.

This fallacy is very similar to the faulty appeal to authority. If it is wrong to appeal to someone who isn't an authority, then it is just as wrong to appeal to many people who are not authorities. The general public is rarely a proper authority on any subject.

> POLITICAL CANDIDATE: My opponent thinks this war is killing innocent people despite the fact that a recent poll concluded 76 percent of Americans think it's okay.

The general public is not an authority on moral issues like this. This is an appeal to the people.

> "This new book, *The Fallacy Detective*, must be the best logic book around. It has been on the best-seller list for months."

We should all know that the most popular book isn't necessarily the best book. This is an appeal to the people.

> "It looks as if more people vacation in Florida than any other place. It must be the nicest place in America to visit."

If more people vacation in Florida, we might be able to say it is *a nice* place to visit. But, we can't say it is *the nicest* place to visit. People might vacation in Florida because it is cheaper – although they really want to go to Hawaii.

This fallacy is covered again in Lesson 32, under the title *bandwagon*.

Illustration by Tim Hodge.

Ladybug is the lone supporter of this idea.
She can't be right.

Exercises

What form of bad reasoning, if any, do you find in the following examples? If there is no bad reasoning, write "none."

1. JENNY: I'm worried about the economy. I think we are entering a depression.
   BERT: I wouldn't worry. I heard that 89 percent of Americans believe the economy is improving.

2. CLYDE: I believe in reincarnation.
   JENNY: Why do you believe in reincarnation?

CLYDE: Shirley MacLaine is very famous, and she has written many books on the subject, and she believes in it.

3. CLYDE: I believe in reincarnation.
JENNY: Why do you believe in reincarnation?
CLYDE: Shirley MacLaine is very famous and has written many books on the subject. She wouldn't have sold any copies if it wasn't true.

4. JENNY: What's the capital of South Dakota?
BERT: The guy at the library said it was Tulsa, but I didn't believe him. It didn't look like he worked there.

5. "What! You're telling me to go on a diet? What about you? You're seventy-five pounds overweight."

6. "My uncle is a child psychologist and pediatrician. He says you shouldn't spank children when they are bad. He says it's ineffective."

7. "We need to give a large subsidy to farmers. The price of corn is so low right now that farmers are going broke. They are being forced to sell their land to pay for their debts. If this keeps up, most of the small, family-owned farms will disappear and we will be left with only large factory farms."

8. "Every developed nation in the world has strict controls on firearms except America."

9. "Everybody's buying these new llama wool coats. They must be warm."

10. "This song has been on the top of the charts for over a month. It must be a very popular song."

11. "It's okay to walk on Mr. Jones's property without asking him. Last week, when I was over there, I met a bunch of boys in the orchard eating apples. People walk on Mr. Jones's land all the time without asking him."

Lesson 12

Straw Man

The fallacy of *straw man* is changing or exaggerating an opponent's position to make it easier to refute.

MOTHER: I think you have been playing too many of those video games lately.

SON: Oh, so you think I should just throw away my $1,000 video game collection and sit up in my room taking practice IQ tests all day?

This is not what the mother said. The son is exaggerating his mother's viewpoint. She thought he should play fewer video games – not no video games at all. The son committed the straw man fallacy.

The straw man fallacy distorts an opponent's position just enough to make it weak. The new argument that is created is called a "straw man" because it is easy to knock down. ("I'll huff and I'll puff and I'll blow your argument down.") The original argument was not as easy to knock down.

POLITICAL CANDIDATE A: Due to this year's budget problems, I think our state should decrease the amount of money going to schools. This would solve the problem. We could bring the amount of money back to normal next year.

POLITICAL CANDIDATE B: My fellow citizens, is this what you want in a candidate? Someone who is against our schools, against our children's education, and against our future?

Candidate B created a straw man argument, and then attacked it. Candidate A only wanted to spend less money on the schools for one year, but Candidate B distorted this to mean Candidate A was against all education. It is much easier to refute someone who is against all education than it is to refute someone who wants something much more mild, such as decreasing spending on schools for one year.

MRS.: Our car isn't running right. I think we need to buy a better one – something more comfortable.

MR.: Oh, so you want us to buy a brand new fancy car? I don't think we have enough money for a Rolls Royce.

Mrs. is not saying she wants a fancy car. She only wants one that is more comfortable and reliable. Mr. is distorting Mrs.'s desires and is creating a straw man argument.

PARENT: Your mother and I have decided that we don't want you to date when you are this young. And when you are old enough, we believe there should be some parental supervision.

DAUGHTER: Oh, now I understand. You're going to make me sit up in my room all my life until you pick out somebody for me to marry.

We should not assume the worst about someone's beliefs. We should take the time to find out what they mean by what they say.

The straw man fallacy is similar to the red herring fallacy. A straw man argument introduces an irrelevant position – a position which nobody in the argument really believes in – then attacks it.

Illustration by Rob Corley.

Do I have to take a bath every time I come in the door?

Exercises

What form of bad reasoning, if any, do you find in the following examples?

1. BERT: I've been learning about the Second World War lately. I found that America provoked Japan into attacking Pearl Harbor. I don't think that was the right thing for us to do.
   JENNY: Oh, so you are now taking the side of the Axis? Do you think Germany and Japan were right to do what they did?

2. "This new book, *The Fallacy Detective*, must be a very popular book. It has been on the best-seller list for months."

3. "Recent polls indicate that millions of Americans are now concerned that global warming will put Los Angeles underwater in twenty years. Shouldn't you be concerned also?"

4. "Nearly everyone I know thinks Caitlin is a liar."

5. "The Supreme Court right now is deciding whether it is right to execute insane people who have committed murder. I think it is all right to execute insane people. If we ban executions of insane people, then everybody on death row will suddenly decide they are insane and purposely fail sanity tests. It would result in chaos."

6. CLYDE: I don't think the North had any right to invade the South during the Civil War.
   SARAH: I can't believe you said that. Slavery was cruel and brutal. Saying the slaves should have been ignored is wrong. The slaves should have been freed immediately.

7. "There can't be any global warming going on. I've asked about ten people today whether they thought there was global warming, and they all said there probably wasn't."

8. "Religion is a bunch of baloney. It all comes from chemical reactions in the brain."

9. MAN ON THE STREET: I'm opposed to capital punishment.
   MAN ON THE SIDEWALK: Oh, you people who oppose punishing criminals make me sick. Don't you ever think about the poor victims at all?

10. "The local talk show host said yesterday that we are on the verge of nuclear war. I think I'm going to sit in my basement for the next couple of weeks."

11. "I wouldn't worry about a little cheating on Tuesday's test if I were you. The test format makes it so easy for you to do a little cribbing, and everybody else does it."

Making Assumptions

Illustration by Rob Corley.

Lesson 13

The Story of Aroup Goupta

Read the following story about Aroup Goupta very carefully. (You must roll the "r" to pronounce the name "Aroup" correctly.) Assume that what is said in this story is all true, and that no one in the story is lying or saying anything which is false. At the end of the story, we will ask you some questions about the story.

The Story of Aroup Goupta

The cat sat there wide-eyed and speechless – as much as a cat can be speechless – for a moment, and then bounded away.

Aroup continued to the end of the alley and turned left. He was now in the most densely populated part of the capital city. He was in a marketplace, and vendor stalls ran along both sides of the street. Aroup heard a vendor chanting in a singsong, "Beets. Fresh beets. Fresh beets for sale."

Aroup was hungry. But he had only two papushkas – the currency used in Clovnia – in his pocket. He did not have enough to buy any food.

"Which way is the center of town?" Aroup asked the dusty-looking vendor.

The man looked up and motioned with his arm.

"Down zat vay," he said.

Aroup continued down the street. He wondered, again, where he would stay the night.

"Lief is a cursed city in a cursed country," he muttered to himself.

It was now growing hotter, and Aroup was forced to take off his woolen sweater. As he did so, Aroup glanced to his left. A man with a large bushy moustache was motioning to him from a doorway.

"Come here. I am a friend," the man said. He motioned again, urgently.

Illustration by Rob Corley.

Aroup went over to him. He remembered he must be careful to whom he talked.

The man grabbed Aroup by the shoulders and whispered in his ear, "My life and yours are not vorth a plug papushka if vee are seen. Hurry!" He pulled Aroup through the door.

The room Aroup entered was dimly lit, compared with the outside.

"Hurry," the man said again, and this time he pulled up a chair next to a booth and pushed Aroup into it. "I vill bring you oatmeal."

As his eyes became accustomed to the dark, Aroup saw that he was in a restaurant. The ceiling was low, and the room smelled of mothballs and stale pipe tobacco. In the center of the room, a dozen short men clustered around a table, drinking beet juice.

Presently, the man with the moustache returned carrying a plate of cold oatmeal.

"You must eat zis slowly," he said. "Tonight you vill stay here."

Aroup obliged, for he was very hungry. The oatmeal, though it was cold and tasted terrible, felt good in his stomach.

The man with the moustache sat down next to him and said something that must have been in the Cloveneeze language.

"Oum av humby av a fpup pib," the man said.

"What was that?" Aroup said. "Are you a native Clovnian?"

"Only native Clovnians can speak Cloveneeze," the man said in English. "It vas very hard to find you. Have you been here long, Aroup Goupta?"

"No," Aroup responded. "I came here yesterday."

"Then you do not know the news?"

Aroup had heard no news since arriving.

What the news was, the little man with the moustache never said, for at that very moment the doors burst open, and several tall men in uniforms strode in, brandishing clubs.

A tall, uniformed man, evidently the leader of the group, strode into the middle of the room and removed a Popsicle from his mouth.

"Ver is de sympathizers?" he said. He spoke not in the common Cloveneeze, but the more coarse French.

All the short men at the table froze for a moment and then rushed for the door.

Aroup was on his feet and was about to follow the short men to the door, when he felt something on his arm. He looked over, to see not the man with the moustache, but a tall woman.

"Follow me," she said and led him out a door at the back of the room.

"Here," the woman said, "take this." She handed Aroup a cat. "You must go through those doors. Behind them is an alley. Go down the alley until you are out of sight." The woman gave him a push and disappeared.

Aroup opened the doors and walked through, clutching the cat. He found himself in the dark alley. He stood there for a moment, wondering what to do. "I wish this all was just a bad dream." The cat hissed, and Aroup dropped it on the ground. He put his sweater back on.

The cat sat there wide-eyed and speechless – as much as a cat can be speechless – for a moment, and then bounded away.

Aroup continued to the end of the alley and turned left. He was now in the most densely populated part of the capital city. He was in a marketplace, and vendor stalls ran along both sides of the street. Aroup heard a vendor chanting in a singsong, "Beets. Fresh beets. Fresh beets for sale…"

Exercises

Read the following statements, and indicate whether (a) you think the statement is true or (b) you don't know if the statement is true. In your answers, stick to what you know was said in the story. As you answer each exercise, check your answer. You can look back at the story if you need to.

1. Aroup Goupta was a man, not a woman.

    true ☐   *don't know* ☐

2. Aroup was in a city.

    true ☐   *don't know* ☐

3. Aroup was in a capital city.

    true ☐   *don't know* ☐

4. Aroup was in a country called Clovnia.

    true ☐   *don't know* ☐

5. Aroup was in the most densely populated part of the city.

    true ☐   *don't know* ☐

6. Aroup was probably a foreign journalist who had come to investigate the political unrest in the country.

    true ☐   *don't know* ☐

7. Aroup had a sweater with him.

    true ☐   *don't know* ☐

8. Aroup was over twenty-five years old.

   true ☐   *don't know* ☐

9. The man with the moustache was Aroup's friend.

   true ☐   *don't know* ☐

10. The man with the moustache pulled Aroup into a restaurant.

    true ☐   *don't know* ☐

11. The man with the moustache spoke Cloveneeze.

    true ☐   *don't know* ☐

12. The man with the moustache was a native Clovnian.

    true ☐   *don't know* ☐

13. The man with the moustache could have worked at the restaurant.

    true ☐   *don't know* ☐

14. The short men were drinking beet juice.

    true ☐   *don't know* ☐

15. The leader of the uniformed men wanted to know where the sympathizers were.

    true ☐   *don't know* ☐

16. The short men at the table were afraid of being arrested as "sympathizers."

    true ☐   *don't know* ☐

17. Aroup thought the oatmeal tasted terrible.

    true ☐   *don't know* ☐

18. Aroup ate the oatmeal.

    true ☐   *don't know* ☐

19. Aroup was too young to be in a restaurant where they served beet juice.

    true ☐   *don't know* ☐

20. The tall woman wanted to save Aroup.

    true ☐   *don't know* ☐

21. Aroup escaped in the nick of time.

    true ☐   *don't know* ☐

22. This is the story that never ends.

    true ☐   *don't know* ☐

Lesson 14

Assumptions

In the previous lesson, we told you the story of Aroup Goupta, and then we asked you questions about the story. You may have given wrong answers to some of the exercises because you thought the story said something which it actually did not say. This lesson aims to show you the value of being aware of your assumptions.

Which Letter Is Different?

Illustration by Rob Corley. (We are grateful to David Pratt for this illustration.)

In the preceding diagram, which of the alphabet letters is different from all the others? (The letter which looks like a "9" is actually a lowercase "Q.")

"a" This letter is different in that it is the first letter of the alphabet. It is the only letter made with a short stem on the right. It is the only vowel.

"b" This letter is different in that it is the only letter with a stem on the left of the circle, not on the right. It is the only letter made with its stem pointing upward.

"c" This letter is different in that it is the only letter with a break in its circle instead of a stem. It is the only letter which is made of only one part.

"q" This letter is different in that it is the only letter which does not follow the others in consecutive alphabetical order. It is the only one which is made with its stem pointing downward.

Do you think that we could make an argument for each individual letter being more different than the others? Is there something you are missing about this picture? Have our questions influenced you to make an assumption which is not true?

What about the "t" in the middle? Did you miss this letter? It is larger than all the others. It is in the center of the diagram. It is made with two straight lines and no curved part.

Did the questions we asked about the diagram cause you to ignore an obvious part of the diagram? Assumptions can be dangerous things when we are not aware of them.

Riddles

At the County Fair, there was a line of stalls displaying all the champion farm animals. One afternoon, during the fair, a man wearing a black vest walked up to the prize Jersey cow, shot her, and then ran out of the display barn. Even though there was a crowd of people around, no one tried to follow the man in the vest. Why was this?

Dr. Taylor lives in Chicago. He had a speaking engagement in St. Louis. He and his wife drove there in the morning. When the lecture was over that evening, they got in their car and continued to drive in the same direction which they had driven earlier that day. They returned home that night, about six hours after leaving the lecture hall. How can this be?

We will tell you the answers to these riddles soon. Be patient.

Being Aware

An *assumption* is something taken for granted or accepted as true without proof.

This whole section – especially this lesson – is about how people make assumptions without being aware of them. When two people argue, they may have different assumptions. If they knew what they were assuming, then they might realize why they were wrong or why they both actually agreed.

To be aware of assumptions, you need to learn a healthy sense of suspicion – suspicion of everybody, including yourself. If someone is deceived, he is thoroughly convinced that he is not deceived – he does not know what his assumptions are. How can we make ourselves aware of our assumptions? We can't. No one can be totally objective. We can only try to be as objective as we can.

Here are three suggestions on how to be objective:

1. Listen. Every time we listen to someone else's viewpoint, we give ourselves the opportunity to become undeceived.
2. Evaluate our assumptions. It is important to recognize that everyone has a bias and that we need to understand and to manage our own biases. We need to be aware of the assumptions that we are making. Keep asking, "Why do I think this is true?" There is nothing wrong with having assumptions, just as long as we have the correct assumptions.
3. Evaluate other people's assumptions. We should be alert to clues in what people say which may show their assumptions. This will give us insight into why they believe what they believe.

Answers

The man shot the Jersey cow with his camera. He was a journalist for the county newspaper, and he was in a hurry because he had a deadline. Did you have assumptions about what "shot" meant? Did you interpret "shot" to mean that the man in the vest killed the Jersey cow?

Dr. Taylor lives in Chicago, but he did not leave for the lecture from Chicago. He was staying south of St. Louis that morning, and he and his wife drove north to St. Louis to his speaking engagement. Afterward, they continued driving north to Chicago, which is about six hours from St. Louis. When we said that Dr. Taylor lived in Chicago, did you assume that he started his drive from Chicago? Be careful of those nasty little assumptions!

Exercises

A. BRENT: Mom, if you buy that expensive toaster, we won't be able to go out for ice cream after lunch. It's my birthday, and I want to have ice cream.

Based on the paragraph above, Brent is probably assuming which of the following:

1. There is a limited supply of money in his mom's purse.

   yes ☐   *no* ☐

2. He gets to have what he wants on his birthday.

   yes ☐   *no* ☐

3. All toasters are expensive.

   yes ☐   *no* ☐

4. There is no such thing as free ice cream.

  yes ☐   *no* ☐

5. His mom didn't buy ice cream for him the day before and put it in the freezer.

  yes ☐   *no* ☐

6. Ice cream melts when you put it in a toaster.

  yes ☐   *no* ☐

B. Answer the following riddles. See if you can catch the hidden assumptions.

7. Mrs. White, the housekeeper, swept the Blackhurst mansion. She swept all the dust and dirt in the rooms into five different piles around the house – two upstairs and three downstairs. Then she asked Bidwell, the butler, to help her sweep all the piles together. How many piles of dust will they have?

8. Why are 1996 U.S. pennies worth more than 1967 U.S. pennies?

9. Answer each of these riddle questions, and then check your answers at the end:

a. What color is snow?

b. What color is the opposite of black?

c. What color is a boiled egg if you take out the yolk?

d. What color are most clouds on a peaceful summer's day?

e. What color is the largest part of people's eyes?

f. What color is the circle above?

g. What color are most clothes when you bleach them?

h. What color cloth commonly keeps you the coolest in the hot sun?

i. What do cows drink?

Lesson 15

Circular Reasoning

An argument which says "P is true because Q is true, and Q is true because P is true" is using *circular reasoning.*

There were once two little boys who wanted to eat a cookie together. But each of their mothers had said that they couldn't have any.

SAM: I've got an idea. Why don't I take a cookie from my mother's jar, and we can share it? Then, Bill, you'll take a cookie from your mother's cookie jar and put it in my mother's jar.

BILL: But then I will get in trouble 'cause my mom will see a cookie gone.

SAM: Then we can take a cookie from my mom's jar and put it in your mom's jar, so she won't notice.

BILL: No, then you will get in trouble.

SAM: I don't get it. We're going in circles here.

This is circular and isn't getting these boys anywhere.

PLAINTIFF: Judge, I'm not lying. I'm a religious person, and religious people don't lie.

JUDGE: How do I know you are a religious person?

PLAINTIFF: Because I would never lie.

The plaintiff is using circular reasoning. The plaintiff is saying that he is a religious person, and since religious people don't lie, he isn't lying. We have to assume that he isn't lying when he says he is a religious person! The plaintiff is going in circles, which is why this is called circular reasoning.

The plaintiff is essentially saying "P is true because Q is true, and Q is true because P is true" or "It's true because it's true." Circular arguments assume the thing they are trying to prove. Some circular arguments can be very difficult to catch and unravel. They make you feel like you want to take your brain out and look at it.

PEANUTS reprinted by permission of United Feature Syndicate, Inc.

Circular reasoning. Girls are smarter because scientists have proven it. We know the scientists are right because they are girls, and girls are smarter.

JIMMY: Dad, why do I have to learn logic?
DAD: Because it will help to develop your mind.
JIMMY: Why will it develop my mind?
DAD: Because it will help you think better.

Jimmy's dad is using a very simple circular argument. He is simply repeating his first statement but using different words to say the same thing. Jimmy wants more proof, but his dad won't give it. He did not actually answer his son's question. Sometimes when someone can't think of a better argument for something, he simply restates his original argument in different words as proof for his old argument.

When someone tries to support an argument by just repeating his main premise, then he is using circular reasoning. If we said that "everyone should study logic because logic should be studied by everyone," we would be using circular reasoning.

"To allow every man unbounded freedom of speech must always be, on the whole, advantageous to the state; for it is highly conducive to the interests of the community that each individual should enjoy a liberty, perfectly unlimited, of expressing his sentiments." – Richard Whately, *Elements of Logic*, 1826

This is a classic example of circular reasoning. Many famous and intelligent men have used circular reasoning like this without realizing it – and many others have used circular reasoning and did know that they were using it. Sometimes we are so captured by the magic of words that we never realize that an argument only went in a circle.

Exercises

A. Which of the following examples contain the fallacy of circular reasoning?

1. PERSON A: Capital punishment for murder is perfectly justified.
   PERSON B: Why is that?
   PERSON A: Because it is right for society to put to death those who have committed murder.

   circular   *not circular*
   reasoning   *reasoning*

2. POLITICIAN RUNNING FOR PUBLIC OFFICE: You can all trust what I say. I have never lied in my life.

   circular   *not circular*
   reasoning   *reasoning*

3. WOMAN: It doesn't seem like you love me.
   MAN: Why is that?
   WOMAN: If you loved me, you would give me all your money.

   circular   *not circular*
   reasoning   *reasoning*

4. "You shouldn't pray to your dead ancestors because they're dead. But you should pray to God because you couldn't pray to him if he didn't exist."

   circular   *not circular*
   reasoning   *reasoning*

5. A: I feel that astrology brings us closer to the truth about our future, don't you?
   B: No. I think it's stupid.

A: But I know it is true because I'm an Aries, and people born under the sign of Aries are very good at discovering the truth.

circular reasoning ☐   *not circular reasoning* ☐

6. TEENAGER: Who took my hairbrush? I never can find it when I want it, and when I don't want it, it's always right there.

circular reasoning ☐   *not circular reasoning* ☐

7. PERSON WHO WANTS TO STUDY LOGIC BUT HASN'T YET: I know that all the people who want to study logic are very intelligent people. It's very simple. If they weren't so intelligent, then they wouldn't want to think logically! Obviously.

circular reasoning ☐   *not circular reasoning* ☐

8. HUSBAND: I'm tired. When we get home I'm going to sit and relax and eat in front of the TV. That's what I need to do.
WIFE: And I suppose I'll have to work my fingers to the bone cooking that food you're going to eat...
HUSBAND: Why, who else would do it?

circular reasoning ☐   *not circular reasoning* ☐

9. NEWS REPORTER AFTER A DEBATE: My fellow Americans, these debates have given you the opportunity to observe a pessimistic candidate who nearsightedly hearkens us back to the defeatism and uncertainty of four years ago. You have also observed an inspiring, future-oriented optimist who believes in the strength and hope of America and who wants to continue moving us forward. I am confident you will let your wisdom be clearly known at the polls.

circular reasoning ☐   *not circular reasoning* ☐

10. PROFESSOR SNEEDELL: All experts in this field agree with my findings.
    STUDENT: But I heard that Professor Schilling disagrees with you.
    PROFESSOR SNEEDELL: He isn't an expert, so his views don't count.
    STUDENT: How do you know he doesn't have any experience in this field?
    PROFESSOR SNEEDELL: Obviously he must not have any experience, since he disagrees with me.

circular reasoning		*not circular reasoning*	

11. "We must accept the traditions of the men of old time who affirm themselves to be the offspring of the gods – that is what they say – and they must surely have known their own ancestors. How can we doubt the word of the children of the gods?" – Plato, *Timaeus*

circular reasoning		*not circular reasoning*	

B. What fallacy, if any, is committed in the following examples?

12. ADVERTISEMENT: Taylor Swift brushes her teeth with Colgate.

13. YANKEE: Yuck! You're eating grits! I don't see how you can stand them – they originated in the South, and southern foods taste terrible.

14. "Handgun Control, Inc. says buying a gun will make you suicidal. I don't think I'll buy a gun. Those people at Handgun Control, Inc. must be experts on guns."

C. Is there an example of circular reasoning in the following dialogue? If so, what is it?

15. LITTLE GREEK: I think I have a cold.

BIG GERMAN: At least it isn't an echinacea cold.

NOSY AUSTRIAN: What is an echinacea cold?

BIG GERMAN: You take echinacea because you think you might be catching a cold. Then when you stop taking it, you get an even worse cold because you've stopped.

NOSY AUSTRIAN: What clinical studies have led you to believe this theory?

BIG GERMAN: I know it's true because it happened to me.

NOSY AUSTRIAN: But anecdotal evidence, especially just from one experience, isn't reliable.

LITTLE GREEK: Real doctors don't recommend taking echinacea.

NOSY AUSTRIAN: How do you know that? What are "real" doctors?

LITTLE GREEK: Real doctors who go to college know more than those health-nut doctors like Dr. D—, who recommends taking herbs because he sells them.

NOSY AUSTRIAN: How do you know the difference between a real doctor and the other kind?

LITTLE GREEK: Because real doctors are smarter.

NOSY AUSTRIAN: How do you know that the IQ of doctors who do not recommend taking echinacea is higher than doctors who do recommend taking echinacea? Have you done studies on the different IQs of doctors?

LITTLE GREEK: It's obvious they are smarter. They don't recommend taking echinacea.

NOSY AUSTRIAN: Our argument is going in a circle.

LITTLE GREEK: No, it isn't.

Lesson 16

Equivocation

Somebody walks up to you and punches you in the nose. Now, this isn't normal behavior, so you ask the offender, "Ow! Why'd you do that?"

He responds, "Today is Tuesday, and I can't stop myself from doing that on Tuesdays. I have a habit."

Not satisfied, you say, "So, what does that have to do with anything?"

"Well," he says, "everybody is in the habit of doing something. You are probably in the habit of brushing your teeth in the morning. You're probably also in the habit of buckling your seat belt when you take a ride in a car. So, I see nothing wrong with my little habit."

Now, we all smell that something fishy is going on with this story. Where is it coming from? The arguer is playing with his words. He is changing the meaning of the word "habit."

When he begins, "habit" means something someone does because he lacks self-control. He says, "I can't stop myself from doing that on Tuesdays. It's a habit." Habit, here, refers to things like biting your nails, cracking your knuckles, or perpetually checking to see if your socks match. Later in the conversation, "habit" refers to something somebody is accustomed to doing often but which is not bad. Getting up in the morning, eating breakfast, etc., are habits.

An *equivocation* changes the meaning of a word in the middle of an argument.

Sometimes the person who commits an equivocation isn't aware of it.

"If the English don't drive on the right side of the road, what are they doing on the wrong side?"

Here, "right" changes meaning from right-hand versus left-hand, to right versus wrong.

> "We must indeed all hang together, or, most assuredly, we shall all hang separately." – Benjamin Franklin at the signing of the Declaration of Independence.

"Hang" changes meaning here from "keeps close company" to "being strung at the end of a rope."
Equivocation is also used for humor.

> DOROTHY: Are you doing that on purpose, or can't you make up your mind?
> SCARECROW: That's the trouble. I can't make up my mind. I haven't got a brain. Just straw.
> DOROTHY: How can you talk if you haven't got a brain?
> SCARECROW: I don't know. But some people without brains do an awful lot of talking, don't they?
> DOROTHY: Yes, I guess you're right.

The Scarecrow is changing the meaning of "brain." First, he is talking about someone who lacks a physical organ called a brain, and later he is talking about somebody who lacks wisdom or sense.

> "Everyone knows that laws change all the time. Prohibition was repealed after only a few years. Laws against criticizing the president were repealed. You see, the laws of thermodynamics, which say that it is impossible to make a true perpetual motion machine, can easily change, just like prohibition. My company is attempting to build a perpetual motion machine. I encourage you to invest in it."

This argument may sound convincing, until you look closely. The speaker first refers to law as a piece of legislation which is made by the government – such as the Constitution or a speed limit ordinance. Then, he refers to law as a natural law, something in nature that never changes – such as the law of gravity.

An equivocation. Hobbes's definition of "peck"
is different than the math book's definition.

Exercises

A. What are the terms which have changed their meanings in these examples?

1. DAD: Go put the dogs in the pen.
   SON: Aw, Dad, I couldn't do that. The dogs are too big. Besides, it would mess up all the ink, and the pen wouldn't write correctly.

2. DAD: Son, when you grow up, I want you always to be a responsible young man.
   SON: But, Dad, I am already very responsible. Whenever something breaks around here, it seems like I am always responsible.

3. COMMUNIST PARTY SPEAKER: The Declaration of Independence says that "all men are created equal." But we see today anything but equality. The rich politician and businessman gorge themselves on luxuries, while poor people pick up trash out of the gutter. Nobody could say that is

equal. Vote for the Communist Party and live up to the intentions of the Declaration of Independence.

4. "Apes, dolphins, and my dog Buster are all intelligent animals. They can all learn to do tricks and learn to have complicated social lives. I think it is wrong to say that man is the only intelligent being."

B. What fallacy, if any, is committed in the following examples?

5. TEENAGER: I'm hungry. I wonder if there is something to eat in the refrigerator....Only leftover roast beef. I guess I'm not that hungry.

6. "Anybody who uses lots of fallacies has got to be very illogical. The book *The Fallacy Detective* uses lots of fallacies (as examples), so it must be a very illogical book."

7. "It is easy to prove that smoking causes cancer, because it has been shown conclusively that smoking is a carcinogenic agent."

8. "Achoo! I must have a cold. Maybe I had better put on a sweater."

9. CLYDE: Good grief, I've been working every day for two weeks straight.
BERT: Why don't you tell your boss that you want a raise because you

work so hard?

CLYDE: I can't get in touch with him. He's on vacation.

10. "Half this game is ninety percent mental." – Yogi Berra

11. COMPUTER: This program has performed an illegal operation and will be terminated.

JENNY: Ahhhh! I'm a criminal! Are they going to throw me in prison?

12. YOUNG PARENT: My uncle says you shouldn't give kids time-outs. He says it's ineffective. My uncle must be right; he works as an electrical engineer, and he is pretty smart.

13. ADVERTISEMENT: This university is the best place to go to school. After all, there is no better place than U of DB to find great friends, learn to improve yourself, and accomplish the great things you are capable of doing.

14. "Who did you pass on the road?" the King went on, holding out his hand to the Messenger for some hay.

"Nobody," said the Messenger.

"Quite right," said the King. "This lady saw him too. So of course Nobody walks slower than you."

"I do my best," the Messenger said in a sullen tone. "I'm sure nobody walks much faster than I do!"

"He can't do that," said the King, "or else he'd have been here first!"
– Lewis Carroll, *Through the Looking-Glass*

Lesson 17

Loaded Question

When someone asks two questions, but one is hidden behind the other, that's a *loaded question*.

"Gimme dat." Four-year-old Bridget grabs a toy shovel from her brother Sam.

"Oughhhhhh!" Sam grabs after the fleet form of Bridget. "Give me back my shovel…!" He trips, sprawling on the sandy beach.

Scurrying like a crab, she giggles, "I want it." Running after her, Sam throws a handful of sand at Bridget, still out of reach.

Bridget stops and hurls the shovel in Sam's direction, wailing, "Mawwww, Sam took my shovel and got sand in my eyes. Waaaaahhhhhaaahh."

Looking up, Mother asks sharply, "Sam, come here. Why did you take that shovel from your baby sister?"

Mother has asked a loaded question. Her question contained two questions rolled into one. She should have first asked, "Sam, did you take that shovel from Bridget?" before she asked, "Why did you take that shovel from Bridget?" Sam may not have actually taken the shovel from Bridget.

JUDGE: Prosecution, you may now cross-examine the witness.

PROSECUTOR: Mr. Blanchard, what did you use to wipe your fingerprints off this gun?

Illustration by Rob Corley.

DEFENDANT, MR. BLANCHARD: I didn't use anything.

PROSECUTOR: You left your fingerprints on the gun, then?

MR. BLANCHARD: No! I've never seen that gun.

PROSECUTOR: But you just said you never wiped your fingerprints off this gun.

DEFENSE ATTORNEY: Your Honor, the prosecution is trying to confuse my client...

PROSECUTOR: Okay. Let me ask a different question. Mr. Blanchard, have you stopped beating your wife?

MR. BLANCHARD: No.

PROSECUTOR: Have you ever felt guilty for being so abusive to your wife?

MR. BLANCHARD: I never abused my wife.

PROSECUTOR: But you just said you haven't stopped beating her. Any intelligent person on the jury knows that if you still beat your wife, then you are an abusive husband.

MR. BLANCHARD: I never said I beat my wife! You asked...

The prosecution is trying to confuse the defendant by asking loaded questions. These questions contain hidden assumptions, and Mr. Blanchard is having trouble understanding how to answer them. If he answers "yes" to the question "Have you stopped beating your wife," then everybody in the court will think that Mr. Blanchard used to beat his wife. If he answers "no," then everyone will think that he still beats his wife.

The purpose of a loaded question is to make you assume the answer to a hidden question, without actually asking that hidden question.

> POLL QUESTION: Are you in favor of the president's risky new health care plan that has been proven to be inefficient in Europe?

If you respond to this poll, you may not know it, but you answer more than one question. The two questions that should be asked here are: Do you think the president's health care plan is risky and proven to be inefficient? And, are you in favor of it? The people who wrote the question have a hidden agenda – or assumption. They want to convince you that the health care plan is a bad idea. They want you to answer "No!"

When you suspect that someone is asking you a loaded question, then ask yourself how you can split the question. Before answering the question, you need to question the question – be aware of the assumptions behind it.

Exercises

A. Which of the following arguments contain a loaded question? If an argument contains a loaded question, explain what the unstated question is.

1. NEIGHBOR: Why do you like to disturb the neighborhood by playing your music so loud that everybody can hear it a mile away?

    loaded question   *no loaded*
                                         question

2. ADVERTISEMENT: So, when are you going to make the new Ford Bubble-box your first car?

loaded question ☐   *no loaded question* ☐

3. MOTHER TO CHILD: When was the last time you took a bath?

loaded question ☐   *no loaded question* ☐

4. LETTER TO THE EDITOR: I am just furious about the mayor's handling of this new city ordinance designed to protect environmentally sensitive residents. What is he going to do when the state tourism bureau lists us as the worst-smelling city just because thoughtless people are allowed to burn their leaves and make everybody else suffer? The question I'd like to ask the mayor is: what is he going to do when we civic-minded residents protest his actions and start burning our leaves in front of city hall? What's that going to do for his city beautification project?

loaded question ☐   *no loaded question* ☐

5. MAGAZINE AD: Does the pain medication you use now start to work in less than one second?

  loaded question ☐   *no loaded question* ☐

6. COMMERCIAL FOR SECURITY SYSTEM: Can your business run the risk of computer hackers breaking into your most sensitive files?

  loaded question ☐   *no loaded question* ☐

7. CHILD TO MOTHER: Why is the president always so grumpy? Is it because he wanted to be an astronaut instead, but his mommy made him become president?

  loaded question ☐   *no loaded question* ☐

8. PHONE SALESPERSON: Yes, madam, our company sells only the best kitchen utensils.... Yes, we guarantee everything we sell for three days or your money back.... Certainly, we never pressure you to buy more products down the road. What will it be – check, cash, or credit card? I can take any form of payment that is convenient for you...

  loaded question ☐   *no loaded question* ☐

9. PERSON A: You think too much.
   PERSON B: No, I'm just not good at making quick decisions.

   loaded question ☐   *no loaded question* ☐

B. What fallacy, if any, is committed in the following examples?

10. "The Cubs must be a good baseball team. They are very popular in their hometown of Chicago."

11. "Not everyone can be famous because some of us have to be less popular than everybody else."

12. MOM: Do you know where my *Reader's Digest* is?
    JENNY: Did the dog eat it?

13. "It is commonly known that, of all the living creatures on this planet, man is the only rational being. Therefore, we can conclude that women are irrational."

14. "Every time I go to the store, I end up buying something I don't need and forgetting everything I came for."

15. BEAUTIFUL MOVIE ACTRESS: I know you have trouble understanding why the aurora borealis is an ancient civilization of aliens trying to communicate with us. But that's because you're human. Humans can't understand psychic languages.

Lesson 18

Slippery Slope

One cold night, as the little Arab sat in his tent, his camel thrust the tent flap aside.

"I pray thee, master," the camel asked, "let me put my head within, for it is cold."

"By all means, and welcome," said the Arab. The camel stretched his head into the tent.

"If I might but warm my neck also," he said, presently.

"Put your neck inside," said the Arab.

Soon the camel was turning his head from side to side.

"It would take but little room if I put my front legs within the tent. It is difficult standing without."

"You may also put your legs within," said the Arab, moving to make room, for the tent was small.

"May I not stand wholly within?" asked the camel, finally. "I keep the tent open by standing as I do."

"Yes, yes," said the Arab. "You can be warm as well as myself." So the camel crowded into the tent.

But the tent was too small.

"I think," said the camel, "there is not room for both of us. It will be best for you to stand outside, as you are the smaller." With a push, the little Arab made haste to get out.

It is a wise rule to resist the beginnings of evil.

(Adapted from "The Arab and His Camel" from *The Book of Fables and Folk Stories* by Horace Scudder, 1915)

The *slippery slope* fallacy assumes that if we take one step, nothing will stop us from taking a series of steps because each step is the same.

MOTHER: We can't let her get another dog!

FATHER: Oh, we can handle two dogs in the house. She loves animals.

MOTHER: Two dogs? She'll ask for three or four next. This isn't going to stop!

This slippery slope fallacy assumes there is no line between adding one dog to the house and adding two or three dogs. But one dog and three dogs are different. Sometimes the way to recognize a slippery slope fallacy is to take the progression to its logical conclusion.

FATHER: Why stop at three dogs? Maybe she'll ask for a thousand dogs!

MOTHER: That's ridiculous. We couldn't even open the front door.

Illustration by Rob Corley.

A slippery slope

NATIONAL HANDGUN ASSOCIATION: If Congress passes this law requiring trigger locks on guns, next they'll tell us to register our guns. Then they'll know exactly who to confiscate them from. And when only outlaws have guns, they'll have nothing to fear.

Maybe Congress shouldn't require gun owners to use trigger locks. But we shouldn't assume Congress will use a law requiring locks as a precedent for mandatory gun registration. And we shouldn't assume Congress will then confiscate our guns. Or assume that, if they took our guns away, criminals would have nothing to fear. This argument assumes a lot of things that aren't proven. This is a slippery slope fallacy.

Like the story of the Arab and his camel, it's wise to resist the beginnings of evil. But evil may begin when we accept a slippery slope fallacy.

> CAMPER A: Could you change your T-shirt? You've been wearing it all week, and it really smells!
>
> CAMPER B: Why? This shirt was fine on Monday. You had no complaints on Tuesday. No problem Wednesday. All of a sudden something's wrong with it?

The camper with the smelly shirt says that since there's no line, there's no difference. However, just because the neighbor holding his nose can't show precisely when the T-shirt became too smelly for good community relationships, this does not mean the smell never crossed that threshold.

This is a slippery slope fallacy because the smelly camper says there is no difference, no line, no fence. But this is an assumption that needs to be proven. We aren't going to assume there is no difference or that a series of bad things will happen just because it is hard to draw a line.

Exercises

What form of bad reasoning, if any, do you find in the following exercises?

1. CITY COUNCIL MEMBER: If we grant this permit to build this Islamic mosque in our city, it's going to open the floodgates to terrorists! Before we know it, we'll have people planting bombs in City Hall!

2. WIFE: Are you in a bad mood because the Cubs lost last night?

3. LETTER TO A NEWSPAPER: If we let the government implant tracking devices in criminals, it's not going to stop there! They're going to want to track schoolchildren and eventually everybody!

4. For want of a nail the shoe was lost.
   For want of a shoe the horse was lost.
   For want of a horse the rider was lost.
   For want of a rider the battle was lost.
   For want of a battle the kingdom was lost.
   And all for the want of a horseshoe nail.
   – "For Want of a Nail," a medieval proverb

5. "You can't give me a ticket for speeding. I'm the mayor of this town!"

6. SUZY: Can I go over to Mandy's house for an hour?
   MOTHER: If I say yes, you're going to ask if you can stay the night at her house!
   SUZY: Can I?

7. ZACK: I think that some people are nice. I want to find a nice person.
   CLETUS: Oh, no I disagree. I think your argument presupposes a reductive approach to human reason and to the human person. This creates an indissoluble epistemological problem and is ultimately subversive.
   ZACK: Oh, really? I'm sorry; I'll never do it again.

8. CLETUS: Do you believe you exist?
   ZACK: Uhhh, wow! That's a deep question.
   CLETUS: You probably never thought to ask yourself that question. I believe I exist because my entire belief structure is predicated on the fact that I exist.
   ZACK: Wow! You sure are smart!

9. BANK CUSTOMER (IN 1962): Why can he step ahead of me in the line, sir?
   BANK TELLER: He's a white man, and you're a black woman.

10. MRS.: We're not turning the air conditioner on! It's only 89°.
    MR.: I'm dripping!
    MRS.: You didn't complain when it was 80° or 88°. So 89° isn't any different.

11. CLETUS: Do you believe that the sky is blue?
    ZACK: Wow! I think so.
    CLETUS: Ah, but you are wrong. If we define the word "blue" as "three men planting tulips in a garden," then we can definitely say the sky is not blue.
    ZACK: Wow! You're smart!

12. CLARENCE DARROW: If today you can take a thing like evolution and make it a crime to teach in the public schools, tomorrow you can make it a crime to teach it in the private schools, and next year you can make it a crime to teach it to the hustings or in the church. At the next session, you may ban books and the newspapers.... Ignorance and fanaticism are ever busy and need feeding. Always feeding and gloating for more.

Today it is the public school teachers; tomorrow the private. The next day the preachers and the lecturers, the magazines, the books, the newspapers. After a while, Your Honor, it is the setting of man against man and creed against creed until with flying banners and beating drums we are marching backward to the glorious ages of the sixteenth century when people lit torches to burn the men who dared to bring any intelligence and enlightenment and culture to the human mind. – Scopes Monkey Trial, 1925

Lesson 19

Part-to-Whole

When someone says that what is true of part of something must also be true of the whole thing, he is using the *part-to-whole fallacy.*

CHILD: Mommy, why is this feather pillow so heavy? It just has feathers in it, and little feathers don't weigh anything.

Sometimes it is hard for children to understand why a part of something weighs very little, but the whole thing may weigh much more. A million little blades of grass added together in a bale of hay can weigh a ton or more.

JENNY: You won't believe how delicious this chocolate cake is going to be. I'm only using the best ingredients. It has seventeen pounds of imported Dutch chocolate, two hundred and fifty-six candied maraschino cherries, sixty-five organic farm-fresh duck eggs…

Jenny is assuming that the quality of the ingredients in her cake will guarantee the quality of the finished product, but she may never have baked a cake in her life! The quality of the cake may turn out to be very different from the quality of the ingredients.

BART: What on earth are you doing? You look like you are building the Statue of Liberty out of paper clips!
BETH: You guessed it. I've just started. All I have is the structure outlined.
BART: That's a brainless idea – it'll look stupid. Anybody knows you can't make something beautiful out of ugly old paper clips.

Bart thinks that because paper clips are commonplace, therefore anything made from paper clips must also be commonplace. This is the part-to-whole fallacy, where someone thinks that the character of the parts is the character of the whole thing altogether.

> HANS: We know our logic book doesn't have flaws in it because we checked every page and each one is flawless; therefore this is a flawless logic book.
>
> NATHANIEL: If any of our readers finds a mistake in our book, then the printer must have done it.

We know this is true because we logicians are experts at detecting mistakes, and so any book written by a logician can't be mistaken.

Actually that last sentence was also a part-to-whole fallacy. Just because every page in this logic book has no mistakes does not prove that there are not larger mistakes throughout the whole book – for instance a mistake in the order of the lessons or a mistake in the ideas we teach. But we've decided to blame the printer if we find any.

Illustration by Rob Corley.

*They're paper clips! You can't make
something beautiful out of paper clips!*

Exercises

A. Which of the following arguments contain a *part-to-whole fallacy?*

1. JOHNNY: If logicians are experts at organized thinking, does that mean that a convention of logicians would be well organized?

   part-to-whole fallacy ☐   *not part-to-whole fallacy* ☐

2. "Team U.S.A. was selected from the best players in the United States. Since they are all the best at their positions, this team is going to win."

   part-to-whole fallacy ☐   *not part-to-whole fallacy* ☐

3. WRITER: I know why I have writer's block today. It's cloudy outside, and that makes me feel depressed and uncreative.
   CRITIC: Don't let yourself think that way. You'll always be able to think of some excuse for why you don't have to make yourself accomplish something.
   WRITER: Then maybe it's because I started the first part of my day with too big of a breakfast. That can make me feel tired for the whole morning.

   part-to-whole fallacy ☐   *not part-to-whole fallacy* ☐

4. "…the universe is spherical in form…because all the constituent parts of the universe, that is the sun, moon, and the planets appear in this form."
   – Nicolaus Copernicus, *The New Idea of the Universe*

   part-to-whole fallacy ☐   *not part-to-whole fallacy* ☐

5. "Seeing that the eye and hand and foot and every one of our members has some obvious function must we not believe that in like manner a

human being has a function over and above those particular functions?"
– Aristotle, *Nicomachean Ethics*

| part-to-whole fallacy | ☐ | not part-to-whole fallacy | ☐ |

6. ROYAL JESTER: No one laughs at my jokes anymore. It must be because I don't have enough little bells on my hat.

| part-to-whole fallacy | ☐ | not part-to-whole fallacy | ☐ |

7. RICH HUSBAND TO HIS WIFE: Dear, I haven't spared a penny to get the most exquisite materials and furnishings for our new home. I hope you're happy. It's the best house money could buy.
   WIFE: Why does this marble floor in the dining room seem to slope down toward the kitchen? Look! The zebra wood dining table is sliding toward the dumbwaiter! And what are the bronze electrical outlets doing in the vaulted ceiling? How am I supposed to reach them? And why does the hall light switch make all the toilets flush? And what is a smoke detector doing inside the fireplace?

| part-to-whole fallacy | ☐ | not part-to-whole fallacy | ☐ |

8. FARMER: Look at that field of corn. The whole thing looks so perfectly beautiful!

| part-to-whole fallacy | ☐ | not part-to-whole fallacy | ☐ |

9. JOHNNY: Dad, this logic book by the Bluedorn boys has a mistake in it. It says "whole-to-part" here, and it should say "part-to-whole." If the Bluedorn boys are logicians and they don't know how to tell their logical fallacies apart, then I don't think I should be studying logic at all – the whole subject of logic is probably one big mix-up.

| part-to-whole fallacy | ☐ | not part-to-whole fallacy | ☐ |

B. What fallacy, if any, is committed in the following examples?

10. "It would be a crime to pass up another helping of this lasagna. I don't want to go to jail, so I had better have a little more."

11. "What other explanation can there be for all the evidence supporting mental telepathy than the explanation that mental telepathy is human-kind's way of interfacing with the spirit world?"

12. "We all have the obligation to help those who are less fortunate. Not every person can be expected to be rich, and therefore some people need aid from those with better resources."

13. PROSECUTING ATTORNEY: What were you doing on the night of the murder?
    WITNESS: Say, did anybody ever tell you that you have a striking resemblance to Bradley Cooper?

14. "This book on psychology says child rearing should not be done by the parents of the child. It should be done by the government. It says parents harm their children when they try to teach them. What an interesting idea. I didn't know I was hurting my poor little Johnny."

15. CLETUS: Do you believe that life is the absence of death or that death is the absence of life?
    DOMBREZEL: I'm not sure. I think I believe both life and death coexist

on the same spiritual plane, and spirits move back and forth across this plane.

CLETUS: Wow! That sounds very cool.

16. "If you're going to add that much salt to the soup, you might as well pour the whole container in!"

17. WIFE: You signed that petition? You put your name down?
HUSBAND: And my phone number.
WIFE: They're going to call you right up and ask for a donation!

Lesson 20

Whole-to-Part

When someone says that what is true of something as a whole must also be true of each of its parts, then this person is using the *whole-to-part fallacy*.

SPORTS REPORTER: In this year's games, Team America has won more medals than any other team in history. So Jim, who's on Team America, must be a great athlete.

Just because the team as a whole is a good team and wins lots of games doesn't mean each individual player is good. They may all be bad individually but work well together as a team.

This fallacy is the reverse of the part-to-whole fallacy. It's easy to get these two fallacies mixed up – they are so similar.

Part-to-whole

LITTLE WILBER AT THE BEGINNING OF THE FAMILY PICNIC: If I can pull apart one earthworm with my fingers, Mommy, why can't I pull apart a handful of earthworms?

Whole-to-part

LITTLE WILBER AT THE END OF THE FAMILY PICNIC: If our bag of potato chips won't float when I throw it in the pond, why will one of my potato chips float by itself?

Little Wilber doesn't understand that individual earthworms and individual potato chips have different qualities by themselves than when they are in large groups.

Part-to-whole

ANGRY COLLEGE STUDENT: What's wrong with killing people? We humans are just made of all the food we've eaten – digested and made into skin and bones. If I shoot you, I'm just rearranging a bunch of former hamburgers and french fries.

Whole-to-part

GEEKY COLLEGE STUDENT: Mrs. Mempher, this chocolate cake is delicious. What did you put in it?

MRS. MEMPHER: Oh, I included some flour, some chocolate, some sugar, some butter…

GEEKY COLLEGE STUDENT:… Whoa! I have some butter at home! The minute I get home, I'll eat a stick of butter. If this delicious cake has butter in it, then a stick of butter must taste just as good.

The angry college student believes that humans are nothing more than what we eat. But humans are more than just the atoms and molecules which make up our bodies. And the geeky college student thinks that the good taste of the cake as a whole will be the same for each of its ingredients – like the butter.

DILBERT reprinted by permission of United Feature Syndicate, Inc.

Whole-to-part fallacy. Just because scientists in general may be smarter, this does not mean that each individual scientist is smart.

One way to tell the difference between a part-to-whole and a whole-to-part fallacy is to look at the conclusion of the argument. A conclusion which says something about the *whole* is a part-to-whole fallacy. A conclusion which says something about just *part* of the whole is a whole-to-part fallacy.

Exercises

A. Which of the following examples contain a part-to-whole fallacy, a whole-to-part fallacy, or neither?

1. INEPT GUY TRYING TO FIX HIS CAR IN HIS BACKYARD: My car is a General Motors car, so every part must be made by GM.

   part-to-whole fallacy   whole-to-part fallacy   neither

2. SHOPKEEPER: The Smith family has always been hardworking and creative; I don't doubt that Bubba Smith will make a good employee.

   part-to-whole fallacy   whole-to-part fallacy   neither

3. FARMER: I know from experience that this farm can produce about two hundred bushels of corn per acre. I think this area on the side of this hill will be a fertile place to plant our garden.

   part-to-whole fallacy   whole-to-part fallacy   neither

4. POLITICIAN: If each individual person is the best at managing his own interests, then won't society become the most efficient when we maximize individual liberty?

   part-to-   [ ]   whole-   [ ]   neither   [ ]
   whole   to-part
   fallacy   fallacy

5. WOODSMAN HUNTING FOR HIS LOST AX: If I keep searching in this part of the forest, I might never find what I'm looking for.

   part-to-   [ ]   whole-   [ ]   neither   [ ]
   whole   to-part
   fallacy   fallacy

6. NEWSPAPER COLUMNIST: If each American resolves to be more aware of the dangers around us, then we as a society will be able to feel safer in our daily lives.

   part-to-   [ ]   whole-   [ ]   neither   [ ]
   whole   to-part
   fallacy   fallacy

7. NEWS REPORT: Over the past hundred years, the residents of Ikabiki have torn down the royal palace and have taken little parts of it to their homes. They do this in the hope that they can make their homes more elegant with the timbers, hunks of stone, and pieces of iron banister which once made up the most magnificent architectural accomplishment of the Ikabiki civilization.

   part-to-   [ ]   whole-   [ ]   neither   [ ]
   whole   to-part
   fallacy   fallacy

8. A DESPERATE LITTLE AX, LOOKING FOR THE WOODSMAN WHO LOST IT IN THE WOODS: If I just poke part of my handle up a little higher, my master might see me. Oh! He's looking this way!

part-to-whole fallacy ☐   *whole-to-part fallacy* ☐   *neither* ☐

B. What fallacy, if any, is committed in the following examples?

9. FARMER TO HIS FAMILY: Which one of you left the pasture gate open and let all the cows out?

10. MAN: It is well known that men are more intelligent than women since their heads are bigger and thus their brain size is larger. Clearly, then, brain size is correlated with intelligence, since the evidence shows that people with larger brains are also more intelligent.

11. BUSINESSMAN: I don't think I can go wrong to invest in the Pffizt-Hickup Amalgamated Tweezers Factory. Everybody knows the whole economy is booming.

12. "Those are my reasons for doing it, but since you never listen to reason, you'll ignore them."

13. "Everybody's going to see the new movie *The Day of the Spatulas*. It has been the most popular movie for weeks. It must be a movie with a good plot, strong characters, and strong moral values."

14. "The first lady thinks everyone should learn to read and learn to read well. It must be very important."

15. Scientists have discovered something they call the butterfly effect. The idea is that a butterfly flapping its wings in Africa will make tiny changes in air currents, and this may ultimately change the path a tornado might take in Oklahoma.

16. SON: Can I borrow the car to go to the store?
    FATHER: If I let you, you'll come back and ask to borrow it for the weekend! No way!

17. PARENT: If we let Central College raise tuition, pretty soon our children will have to spend $50,000 a semester!

18. PRESIDENT OF STOHL-AND-DELEIGH, ATTORNEYS AT LAW: Harvard Law School is a very prestigious school. I'm sure this new lawyer must be a prestigious person since he graduated from Harvard.

Lesson 21

Either-Or

When someone asserts that we must choose between two things, when in fact we have more than two alternatives, he is using the *either-or fallacy.*

Illustration by Tim Hodge.

PATRICK HENRY: Give me liberty or give me death!

NEWS REPORTER: Don't you think that's a bit extreme?

HENRY: What? That I would be willing to lay down my life for my country?

REPORTER: No. It's just you're shouting in my ear.

HENRY: Your forefathers sacrificed their lives, their fortunes, and their sacred

honor in order to pass their freedoms on to their children – freedoms which
you now enjoy! And you ask me to lower my voice! Have you no shame?

REPORTER: Well, maybe you have a point there, but what about your ultima-
tum? Aren't there any other options?

HENRY: Options! We colonists are about to be shackled hand and foot by that
foul tyrant King George, and you want me to give you options! I tell you that
no choice remains for us today but the choice between fighting for liberty and
death as slaves!

REPORTER: Hey, man, like I can think of a few more options. What about
moving to Tahiti?

HENRY: Give me liberty or give me Tahiti.… Somehow I don't think that one
will go over well with General Washington.

Obviously Patrick Henry's original argument was much different from
this one. But *taken only by itself*, Henry's statement "Give me liberty or give
me death!" sets up a false dilemma between two choices.

When someone tries to use this fallacy, usually one of the options is so
absurd that we are forced to choose the other option. This fallacy becomes
obvious once we realize that there are often more than two choices.

JOHNNY: Either you study logic with me, Dad, or else I won't do it.

DAD: What's this again?

Johnny really isn't trying to prove anything to his dad; he just doesn't want
to do another school subject. Johnny has set up a false dilemma, but his dad
solves it by offering a third alternative:

DAD: There's another option. You either study logic, or you're grounded for a
month. That just about exhausts the alternatives.

Either-or arguments can be manipulative.

RED NOSE: Run dry our water jars do.

LITTLE HAWK: To the river for water we must go.

RED NOSE: Never will the Village of Wigwams let us pass. Kill any who
approach they will.

LITTLE HAWK: Discussed this many times we have.

RED NOSE: Attack the village either we must, or die we will!

LITTLE HAWK: Much pain to our people will this bring.

RED NOSE: But logic what I speak is!

LITTLE HAWK: Isn't there another option?

RED NOSE: Afraid you are!

LITTLE HAWK: Could we give them some beads…or a couple horses…for safe passage?

RED NOSE: Thirsty I am. Fight we must!

LITTLE HAWK: Can we talk normal? This reversed sentence stuff drives me crazy.

Red Nose wants to fight, but Little Hawk thinks there may be alternatives. When a person is strongly committed to a particular viewpoint, he often ignores or suppresses possible alternatives.

DOCTOR TO A DISTRAUGHT WOMAN: I'm afraid your husband will either survive the operation or not. There are no other options.

In this case, when there are truly only two possibilities, then an "either-or" form of argument is not a fallacy.

Exercises

A. Identify which of the following arguments use either-or reasoning and which do not.

1. CORN FARMER TO ANOTHER CORN FARMER: Nobody can make a living growing corn. Either the rain is good and we have lots of corn, but the price is low and we lose money; or else there is a drought, and we don't have any corn to sell, even though the price is high.

    either-or ☐   *not either-or* ☐

2. MAFIA THUGS TO THEIR CAPTIVE: Either yer fer us or yer agin' us. And it don't look like yer fer us. So, we're gonna make sure you don' interfere. Come 'ere, Tony…

   either-or ☐   *not either-or* ☐

3. SOCRATES' WIFE AFTER HEARING SOCRATES WAS CONDEMNED TO DEATH: Those wretched judges have condemned you to death unjustly! SOCRATES: Would you really prefer that I were justly condemned?

   either-or ☐   *not either-or* ☐

4. THE BANDIT SHOUTS INTO THE UPTURNED STAGECOACH: Throw out your valuables, m'ladies, or I shoot!

   either-or ☐   *not either-or* ☐

5. MOTHER TO CHILD: Either you take a bath now, or you take a bath after you are done making those mud pies.

   either-or ☐   *not either-or* ☐

6. NEUROPSYCHOLOGIST: Either a genius is born a genius or his environment makes him that way. A little familiarity with the lives of many of the world's geniuses shows that their environment was not always a good influence. If environment isn't an important factor, we can come to only one conclusion: geniuses are born geniuses.

   either-or ☐   *not either-or* ☐

7. COACH TO HIS TEAM: Nice guys finish last.

   either-or ☐   *not either-or* ☐

8. GARDENER TO HIS APPRENTICE: If you don't water these plants, they'll die!

        either-or ☐   *not either-or* ☐

9. FATHER TO HUNGRY CHILDREN: We're not millionaires around here. Would you like rice with bugs in it, a biscuit with weevils in it, or to go to bed hungry again?

        either-or ☐   *not either-or* ☐

10. GRUMPY OLD LADY: It must have been raining, snowing, sleeting, or hailing earlier because the streets are wet. It couldn't be snow or sleet because it's July. It couldn't be hail because I haven't heard any thunderstorms. So it must have rained.

        either-or ☐   *not either-or* ☐

11. HYSTERICAL MOTHER TO HER HUSBAND: You have to teach the boys logic! If you don't teach them logic, they won't learn how to think! And they'll become hobos and die in prison! Don't you care about your sons?

        either-or ☐   *not either-or* ☐

B. What fallacies, if any, are committed in the following examples?

12. "As our nation enters a new century, what are the most important priorities facing our next president? (1) Saving Social Security, strengthening Medicare, and paying on the debt or (2) implementing a 1.7-trillion-dollar risky tax scheme that overwhelmingly benefits the wealthy?"

13. "I know why I have been in a bad mood for so long. It's because my frame of mind hasn't been good."

14. "Over the years, technology has progressed so that today science can do miracles. We have automobiles, computers, and individually wrapped cheese slices. Yet look at the miracles in the Bible. The same people who praise modern scientific miracles say the miracles in the Bible are impossible. This is a contradiction."

15. "Picasso's paintings must look very beautiful. They are very popular."

16. "It's okay to share copyrighted music files with your friends so they don't have to pay for them. It says so right here in this book on contemporary home design!"

17. COLLEGE PROFESSOR: As an individual, I believe it is good for me to plan and control all the decisions in my life. And that's why I believe, as a society, we should let the government control all aspects of our society.

18. FATHER BEFORE SITTING DOWN TO DINNER: Now, I want to know who took the fingernail clippers and hid them under the couch?

19. MOTHER: It's just one can of beer.
    FATHER: Yeah. That's the start. If we let our son have one beer for his twenty-first birthday, it'll be whisky next. He'll be smoking tobacco before we know it. And then he'll smoke marijuana!
    MOTHER: There is a difference between one beer and being addicted to

drugs.

FATHER: Where? What's the difference?

20. An experiment was done in 1882 at Johns Hopkins where "a live frog can actually be boiled without a movement if the water is heated slowly enough; in one experiment the temperature was raised at a rate of 0.002°C per second, and the frog was found dead at the end of 2.5 hours without having moved." – Edward Scripture, *The New Psychology*, 1897

21. GOVERNMENT OFFICIAL IN A THIRD-WORLD COUNTRY: We should be able to trust this new American economic consultant. He's an American, and America is the land of free enterprise. He can't be a socialist.

C. 22. Which is correct to say:
   a. "The milk the cows *is* drinking is white," or,
   b. "The milk the cows *are* drinking is white"?

Statistical Fallacies

Lesson 22

What Is a Generalization?

We all generalize things. That is, we all make broad comments about a group of people or kind of things.

"No matter what they say, all salesmen don't care a bit about the people they sell to. They just want your money."

We say this because we have met many salesmen, heard from our friends about many salesmen, or been salesmen once ourselves. We don't say this because we have known every salesman personally. We generalize every day, and this is often useful. (See, that last sentence was a generalization.)

We make predictions about what somebody is going to do before he does it, and sometimes we are right.

You are playing a game of Clue with Jenny and Bert. Bert, after one of his turns, lays down his cards with a crooked smile and begins to study the ceiling unconcernedly. You have seen that look before. That means he has the solution, and he is about to win the game. Next turn, he wins.

You knew he would win because you generalized. You noticed that he did those things in past games when he won, and you generalized that he would do the same every time he won at Clue.

Elements of a Generalization

A generalization is composed of samples taken from a class.

A *class* is a group of people or things which all have some common characteristics.

(1) All salesmen (2) all used car salesmen, (3) all jelly beans, (4) all times Bert wins Clue. These are all classes of people or things.

When you examine one or more of the people or things in a class, then you are taking a *sample* of that class.

We examine: (1) one salesman, (2) two used car salesmen, (3) all the jellybeans in a dish, (4) the last four times Bert won Clue. All these are samples of their individual classes.

A *generalization* takes a sample from a class of things, then, using the characteristics from that sample, says something about everything in that class.

If we generalized from the above examples, we might come up with something such as: (1) all salesmen are rich, (2) most used car salesmen are money-grubbers, (3) 22.099 percent of jelly beans in the world are black, (4) every time Bert wins Clue, he looks up at the ceiling in that way.

Unless we know what we are doing, taking samples and making generalizations can be a risky business. When our samples and generalizations are not conducted properly, they are called hasty generalizations.

We will discuss hasty generalizations later.

Strong and Weak Generalizations

1. There is nothing absolutely certain about generalizations – instead, a generalization is either *strong* or *weak*.

Generalizations are useful because we don't need to study every single item within a class before we draw a conclusion about the entire class.

For this year's research project, Bert wants to find out how many politicians in the world are corrupt. Since it is very tedious to examine every politician on the planet to check which ones ever took a bribe, Bert is going to take a sample of three million politicians from all over the world, then generalize from that sample. He finds that every single politician he surveyed took at least one bribe and was therefore corrupt. He concludes that all politicians are corrupt.

Bert is probably satisfied with his results. However, Bert never *really* knows whether his generalization is correct until he examines every single politician. There is always the chance that later he will find a politician who isn't corrupt. Then he would have to change his generalization to "Not *all* politicians are corrupt."

This is why a generalization cannot be true or false; it can be only strong or weak. A strong generalization is one which is more likely to be correct.

2. A generalization relies upon samples of a class. It does not rely upon a study of every single member of the class.

If Bert examined every single politician (the class here is "all politicians"), and found that every one was corrupt, he wouldn't be generalizing when he said, "All politicians are corrupt." He would be stating what he knew to be true.

3. Any generalization must be either adjusted or overthrown by a single contrary case.

If Bert studied three million politicians all over the world and found that they were all corrupt, he might generalize that all politicians are corrupt. But if he later finds a single politician who isn't corrupt (maybe he is living off in the jungle somewhere and didn't show up for the census), he would have to at least modify his generalization. "All politicians are corrupt – *except one* whom I know of." Or better, "*Almost* all politicians are corrupt."

4. A generalization becomes stronger as the sample grows larger and more representative.

A good generalization examines a large sample which reaches to all corners of the class being studied. We'll study this more later.

Illustration by Rob Corley.

Bert, the researcher, finds the last politician on earth.

Exercises

A. Decide whether the following examples are generalizations. Assume the speaker is telling the truth about his findings.

1. "I talked to my boss last Monday, and he yelled at me.
   Josie talked to the boss right after Memorial Day, and he yelled at her.
   Reginald talked to the boss yesterday evening, and he yelled at him.
   Conclusion: the boss always yells at people who try to talk to him."

   generalization ☐   *not a* ☐
                                       generalization

2. "All German Shepherd dogs are ferocious. I have owned four German Shepherds, and they were all ferocious."

   generalization ☐   *not a* ☐
                                            generalization

3. "Every single German Shepherd I have ever seen was kindhearted and gentle. I think the German Shepherd breed is kindhearted and gentle."

   generalization ☐   *not a* ☐
                                            generalization

4. "All dogs have fleas. I just finished examining every single dog in the universe, and they all have fleas."

   generalization ☐   *not a* ☐
                                            generalization

5. "People are living longer, happier lives. Over 767 seniors were asked questions about their health, well-being, financial situation, and general happiness. The study found that about 86 percent of seniors claimed that they felt as if they were living lives which were longer and happier than their parents. Ethel Murdock, 76, of Palm Park, Florida, said: 'My parents lived very hard lives on the farm, even when they were older, but I have it easy now.'"

   generalization ☐   *not a* ☐
                                            generalization

6. "There are parts of Alaska which have a high elevation. Mount McKinley is 20,320 feet high."

   generalization ☐   *not a* ☐
                                            generalization

7. Premise One: All novels by Charles Dickens are boring.
   Premise Two: *Great Expectations* is a novel by Charles Dickens.
   Conclusion: *Great Expectations* is boring.

   generalization ☐   *not a*
                             generalization ☐

8. "Studies have shown that women, on average, earn less than men do."

   generalization ☐   *not a*
                             generalization ☐

9. "The best way to catch a thief is to think like one."

   generalization ☐   *not a*
                             generalization ☐

10. PERSON A: I think Mr. Washington is going to win the presidential election.
    PERSON B: Why?
    PERSON A: I can't think of a single person who is going to vote for someone else, and I have talked with a lot of people.

    generalization ☐   *not a*
                             generalization ☐

11. PERSON A: Mr. Washington is going to win the election.
    PERSON B: Why do you think that. Have you been talking to some more of your friends?
    PERSON A: No. I just remembered – Mr. Washington is the only person running for president.

    generalization ☐   *not a*
                             generalization ☐

12. FARMER MCDONALD: Farmers in the country can't make a dime at farming these days. I haven't made a penny this year.
    FARMER BROWN: That's not true. *The Farmer's Journal* asked four

hundred farmers in California, and almost all of them said they made plenty of money this year.

generalization ☐ 				*not a* ☐
							generalization

13. "If I remember right, the last time the Cubs won the World Series was around 1910. The Cubs haven't won a World Series in almost a century."

generalization ☐ 				*not a* ☐
							generalization

14. "I want to take a trip out west. I think it would be fun. Last year we went to Colorado, and we had a lot of fun."

generalization ☐ 				*not a* ☐
							generalization

B. 15. BONUS: Find an example of a generalization in the newspaper or on television.

Lesson 23

Hasty Generalization

The most common logical fallacy is the *hasty generalization*. Ah, there we go with another generalization.

A *hasty generalization* is generalizing about a class based upon a small or poor sample.

When we buy things, we tend to make generalizations about brands. Out here in the wilds of Illinois, farmers own at least one pickup truck to drive – the major pickup – and several "backup" pickups which serve as lawn ornaments. Every farmer bears allegiance to one brand of pickup over another. Certain farmers are Ford farmers, and others are Chevy farmers. (A growing minority are Dodge farmers.) Each thinks his brand is the best.

And the reason for their allegiance?

"Well," Farmer McDonald will say, "I once owned a Ford, and it was junk. Now I only drive Chevys."

All of Farmer McDonald's experience with Ford trucks has come from this single sample. Is that a good sample from which to judge all Ford trucks? When pressed further, Farmer McDonald will confess that his unfortunate Ford really was fifteen-year-old junk, bought used, and all his subsequent Chevys have been bought new and sold early. So his sample of Ford trucks may not be representative.

Down the road, Farmer Brown has a similar story. "I only buy Ford trucks. I once owned a Chevy, and it was junk." Of course, Farmer Brown's dilapidated Chevy had also seen better days before he nursed it home for the first time.

Maybe Ford trucks are junk. Maybe Chevy trucks are junk. But while Farmer McDonald and Farmer Brown may be right to call their own trucks "junk," they need to see many more trucks before they can accurately say all of the opposition's trucks are junk. Their generalizations are hasty.

Ways People Make Hasty Generalizations

1. Too small of a sample

Hasty generalizations commonly do not take a large enough sample. If our sample is not large enough, then it may not be representative of the class we are studying.

We all know that statistics indicate that tossing a coin will result in it landing on heads half the time and tails half the time. However, this does not mean that if we toss it four times we will see heads twice and tails twice. Even if we toss it a dozen times, we might not see an equal number of heads and tails. In order to actually see the heads and tails even out, we need to toss it many, many more times – say, a hundred or a thousand or more – yet even then we may be off by a few.

Obviously, Farmer McDonald and Farmer Brown did not take large enough samples for their generalizations. The trucks they bought may simply have been duds, or they may have been worn-out secondhand vehicles.

Illustration by Tim Hodge.

It turned out Farmer Brown's sample of Ford trucks was rather small.

2. Not a representative sample

Sometimes the sample for a generalization is large, but it isn't representative of the entire class.

If we wanted to know the eating habits of Italians, it would be very easy for us to study the Italians who live in our town. However, there are many Italians in the world: those who live in America, those who still live in Italy, those who are or aren't in the Mafia, those who are on a diet…

The Italians in our town may not eat the same things as those who live somewhere else. This study could conclude that most Italians eat only spaghetti, when in reality, just those in our town eat only spaghetti. Perhaps Italians everywhere else eat pizza and ravioli. Perhaps we only studied Italians when they ate supper and found that they ate spaghetti then – but the rest of the time they ate Pop-Tarts.

Farmer McDonald and Farmer Brown's trucks also weren't representative of the "average" truck of their kind. There are many kinds of trucks in various states of decay. Their trucks were old and broken down. They would need to see a few examples that were not.

Exercises

A. In the following exercises, answer these questions: (a) Is it a generalization? (b) If so, how large is the sample which is being taken? (c) In your opinion, is the generalization strong or hasty? Why? Assume the speaker is telling the truth about his findings.

1. "All plumbers are brilliant. I know a plumber who can calculate the value of pi to the 289,954th digit."

   generalization ☐   *not a*
                                          generalization ☐

2. "All plumbers are rich. I just went to the international plumbers convention and studied three thousand plumbers there. They all made over one hundred thousand a year."

   generalization ☐   *not a*
                                          generalization ☐

3. "My mom teaches people well. Whenever she explains something to me, I understand it perfectly."

   generalization ☐   *not a*
                                          generalization ☐

4. "Some plumbers are brilliant. I'm a plumber, and I know I'm brilliant."

generalization ☐   not a ☐
generalization

5. "Everything written by Charles Dickens is boring to me. I have read all his novels, and they all put me to sleep."

generalization ☐   not a ☐
generalization

6. "Mr. Carl took some aspirin for a headache. A few minutes later he had an upset stomach. The next two times he had a headache, he did the same thing with the same result. He then decided to not take aspirin for headaches. Instead, he took some other pain reliever, and he did not get an upset stomach. Mr. Carl then started taking aspirin again and found that every time he took it, he had an upset stomach. Mr. Carl concluded that any time he takes aspirin, he will get an upset stomach."

generalization ☐   not a ☐
generalization

7. "A barrel contains one hundred thousand jelly beans. After mixing up the barrel thoroughly (taking care that no jelly beans are squashed), we extract five thousand jelly beans. Five hundred jelly beans are black. Therefore, 10 percent of the jelly beans in the barrel are black."

    generalization   *not a*
                                                  generalization

8. "A satellite survey of all of Colorado determined that the average elevation of the state was 6,806 feet."

    generalization   *not a*
                                                  generalization

9. "Southerners talk fast. I was just on the phone with one, and he sure talked fast."

    generalization   *not a*
                                                  generalization

B. Evaluate these conclusions. Based upon your own knowledge of the subject, decide whether the conclusion is probably true or probably false. If you don't know enough about the subject to decide, then determine what you would need to know before you could draw a conclusion.

> Most McDonald's hamburgers are squashed by the time we get them.
>
> EXAMPLE ANSWER: I think this is probably true. I have been to McDonald's restaurants all over the country, and they always serve squashed hamburgers. Or (if you don't know much about the subject), I would need to see hamburgers at many McDonald's restaurants all over the world before I could decide whether this is true.

10. "Most revolutions are bloody."

    probably true ☐   *probably false* ☐

11. "Mrs. X (pick someone you know) always seems to act happy."

    probably true ☐   *probably false* ☐

12. "Pigs are dirty animals."

    probably true ☐   *probably false* ☐

13. "Hairstylists tend to be talkative."

   probably true ☐   *probably false* ☐

14. "Firstborn children are always willful and tend to be spoiled."

   probably true ☐   *probably false* ☐

15. "I am a below-average typist."

   probably true ☐   *probably false* ☐

16. "Americans make more money than citizens of other countries."

   probably true ☐   *probably false* ☐

17. "Almost all the people who live south of the Mason-Dixon Line speak with a drawl."

   probably true ☐   *probably false* ☐

18. "The more people there are on welfare, the worse the economy becomes."

   probably true ☐   *probably false* ☐

19. "Communist governments end in failure."

   probably true ☐   *probably false* ☐

C. 20. BONUS: Find an example of a hasty generalization in the newspaper
   or television. Look for broad statements ("all," "always," "most," "many")
   and see how well these statements are supported.

Lesson 24

What Is an Analogy?

We are reasoning by *analogy* when we compare two items with each other.

BERT: My dad just bought a new car – it's a Ford.

CLYDE: Oh, really? My dad just bought a new Ford a few months ago. What size engine does yours have?

BERT: V-8.

CLYDE: Ours has a V-8 too. What color is it?

BERT: Blue.

CLYDE: So is ours. Boy, our cars are a lot alike. Ours drives very fast. I wonder if yours does?

BERT: I don't know yet, but if both our cars are so much alike, our new car must be fast too.

Bert is reasoning by analogy.

We are *reasoning by analogy* when we compare two or more items with each other. We notice that these items are the same in one or more ways and conclude that they will be the same in other ways also.

Many useful observations can be gained through reasoning by analogy – if it is done properly.

MR. SMITH: The last time we went to the Joneses' house for dinner, we ate salmon, and we were sick for the rest of the evening. The time before that, when we went to the Joneses', we ate salmon, and we were sick for the whole evening. Now, the Jones family has invited us over again, and they are serving salmon. I'll bet we get sick.

In this analogy, Mr. Smith is comparing the last two times they visited the Jones family with this time.

FIRST EVENING: Visited Jones family…Ate salmon…Got sick.
SECOND EVENING: Visited Jones family…Ate salmon…Got sick.
THIS EVENING: Will visit Jones family…Will eat salmon…

Mr. Smith sees a pattern and fills in the blank with "will get sick."

Analogies – like generalizations – are either strong or weak. As with a generalization, we never *really* know whether our analogy is correct until we actually examine the item in question. We don't *know* if Bert's dad's car is fast until we drive it. We don't *know* if Mr. Smith is going to get sick until that evening is over. Therefore, we can't say an analogy is true or false. We can only say an analogy is strong or weak. A strong analogy is one which is likely to be true.

When examining an analogy, we must not only think of areas where the two items are the same. We must also think of areas where the two items are different. How is Bert's parents' car different from Clyde's parents' car? Maybe Bert's is a large pickup truck and Clyde's is a small sports car. These differences can easily change the strength of an analogy. Two items can have a lot in common and a lot not in common.

Illustration by Tim Hodge.

Bert and Jenny thought being Ford fans
meant they had something in common.

Poetic Analogies

While in this chapter we are mostly dealing with scientific analogies – the kind people use to prove things – there are other types of analogies.

Analogy is also used by authors to make a point.

> "The difference between the right word and the almost right word is the difference between lightning and the lightning bug." – Mark Twain

Here, Mark Twain compares the difference between "the right word and the almost right word" with the difference between "lightning and the lightning bug." He is exaggerating to make his point. Unlike more scientific analogies, poetic analogies are not supposed to be very precise. They are just used to illustrate a point.

Difference between Analogy and Generalization

By now you may be wondering, "What is the difference between an analogy and a generalization?"

Here is a generalization:

Hill Brook College and Valley Knoll College are large colleges. They are both located in conservative towns. They both also happen to be the kind of college you would like to attend. Therefore, all large colleges which are in conservative towns are colleges which you would like to attend.

When we *generalize,* we take a *sample,* then we draw a conclusion about everything in the same class – all large colleges in conservative towns are nice; all blue Fords which have V-8s will be fast; 78 percent of all salmon patties are infected with E. coli, etc.

Here is an analogy:

Hill Brook College is a large college. Valley Knoll College is also a large college. Hill Brook is located in a conservative town. Valley Knoll is also located in a conservative town. You know Hill Brook is the kind of college that you would like to attend. Therefore, Valley Knoll is also the kind of college you would like to attend.

When we draw an *analogy*, we *compare* items with each other, then we draw a conclusion about one item, based on what we know about the other item – Valley Knoll College will be good because Hill Brook is; Bert's parents' car will be fast because Clyde's parents' car is; Mr. Smith will be sick tonight because he was the other nights. We are drawing this conclusion from the *similarities* we have seen between the items we have examined.

Exercises

A. Are these examples analogies, generalizations, or neither?

1. "Curt and Bert are both redheads. They both have freckles. They both live in California. Curt has a really bad temper. Since they are so much alike, Bert must have a bad temper."

    analogy ☐   *general-* ☐   *neither* ☐
                        ization

2. "All of the cities in Ohio that have a large population and a significant crime problem also have a large police force. Therefore, all large cities that have a significant crime problem also have a large police force."

    analogy ☐   *general-* ☐   *neither* ☐
                        ization

3. "My cousin Sylvia is a redhead, and she has a bad temper. My cousin Albert, on my mother's sister's husband's side, is a redhead, and he has

a really bad temper. I'm a redhead, and I have a very bad temper. Everybody with red hair must have bad tempers."

    analogy ☐   *general-* ☐   *neither* ☐
                                ization

4. "My cousin Sylvia is a redhead, and she has a bad temper. My cousin Albert, on my mother's sister's husband's side, is a redhead, and he has a really bad temper. I'm a redhead, and I have a very bad temper. The grocery store clerk has red hair. He must have a bad temper."

    analogy ☐   *general-* ☐   *neither* ☐
                                ization

5. "Communism is like prohibition: it's a good idea but it won't work."
   – Will Rogers

    analogy ☐   *general-* ☐   *neither* ☐
                                ization

6. "The broad mass of a nation…will more easily fall victim to a big lie than to a small one." – Adolf Hitler

    analogy ☐   *general-* ☐   *neither* ☐
                                ization

7. "It seems as if every time I buy a burger at McDonald's, it's squashed. I think McDonald's employees always squash their burgers before they serve them. It's probably a company policy."

    analogy ☐   *general-* ☐   *neither* ☐
                                ization

8. JENNY: Chimpanzees have a larger brain size than either dolphins or dodos, and dolphins are very smart. Therefore, I think you are dumb because you look like a gorilla.

    analogy ☐   *general-* ☐   *neither* ☐
                                ization

9. "This thing of being a hero, about the main thing to it is to know when to die." – Will Rogers

   analogy ▢ *general-* ▢ *neither* ▢
                ization

10. "A man should keep his little brain attic stocked with all the furniture that he is likely to use, and the rest he can put away in the lumber room of his library where he can get it if he wants." – Sherlock Holmes

    analogy ▢ *general-* ▢ *neither* ▢
                 ization

11. "Ex-Professor Moriarty of mathematical celebrity…is the Napoleon of Crime." – Sherlock Holmes

    analogy ▢ *general-* ▢ *neither* ▢
                 ization

12. "Let's say you examine four hundred engineers all over the world, and three hundred have at least eight pens in their shirt pockets. Therefore, you conclude, 75 percent of engineers keep at least eight pens in their shirt pockets."

    analogy ▢ *general-* ▢ *neither* ▢
                 ization

B. Turn these analogies into generalizations. For example, if the analogy is:

   Yesterday was cloudy, and it rained.
   The day before that, it was cloudy and it rained.
   Today is cloudy.
   Conclusion: I think it will rain.

The generalization might be:

   All cloudy days will be rainy days.

13. "The last time it rained, the flowers bloomed.
    The time before that, when it rained, the flowers bloomed.
    The next time it rains, the flowers will bloom."

14. "Texas is a southern state near the ocean, and it has palm trees.
    Florida is a southern state near the ocean, and it has palm trees.
    Louisiana is a southern state near the ocean. I'll bet it has palm trees."

15. "Winning a suit against the government is like getting into a fistfight
    with Tony. They are so big and mean, you could never win."

Lesson 25

Weak Analogy

So how can we tell if an analogy is strong or weak?

1. If the similarities between the items being compared are major and the differences only minor, then that analogy is a *strong analogy*.

Let's say, for example, you are a budding scientist wanting to write your graduate thesis on the long-term effects of Pop-Tarts on humans. The only problem is that you can't find enough people who are willing to eat thirty-four Pop-Tarts a day for one year. So you decide to do the experiment on some kind of animal, hoping the results will be similar.

You pick orangutans. There are a lot of similarities between orangutans and people, at least as far as basic anatomy goes. (HANS: Well, actually, I have been informed that this is not the case, but we'll assume it, so I don't have to come up with another example.) Let's say we are both about the same size and have generally the same digestive systems – these similarities are relevant to our study. However, there are some differences between orangutans and humans. Orangutans tend to be a little hairier and have shorter noses than people. Also, people usually don't dip their fingers into the punch bowl at parties.

But with regard to our experiment, these differences seem minor. The similarities between orangutans and humans are major and the differences probably minor.

If you fed Pop-Tarts to striped cucumber beetles for the proper amount of time, it just wouldn't be the same as if you picked orangutans.

2. If the differences between the items being compared are major and the similarities minor, then we call that analogy a *weak analogy*.

Let's go back to Clyde's and Bert's parents' new automobiles. Suppose their conversation went like this:

> CLYDE: Our new car is a blue Ford. It has a fifteen-gallon gas tank, five cup holders, and a sun roof. It sure drives fast!
>
> BERT: Hey! Our car has all of those things. I'll bet it drives fast too.

Clyde's and Bert's parents' new cars do have many similarities. However, color, size of gas tank, and number of cup holders have little to do with the car's speed on the road. The similarities are only minor. If we found that the two cars differed in ways related to speed – Clyde's car had a large engine and was designed by BMW, while Bert's had a small engine and was made for removing garbage – we might say the differences were major.

The fallacy of *weak analogy* claims that some items with only minor similarities are the same in almost everything else.

Calvin uses a weak analogy. Sparrows and little boys are very different.

Sometimes people come up with very wild analogies.

> CLYDE: I think it is all right for governments in developing countries to execute citizens who don't agree with the government.

JENNY: That sounds terrible!

CLYDE: Hey, if you want to make an omelet, you have to break a few eggs.

Clyde, of course, is being ridiculous. The similarities between a developing nation and cooking breakfast are so minor that it would be a waste of time to mention them.

Exercises

A. Here are some analogies with relevant or irrelevant evidence below each analogy. Does the added evidence strengthen, weaken, or do nothing for the analogy?

> "I bought my last three pairs of hiking shoes at Wilson's Shoe Store, and they all lasted a long time. I just bought another pair of hiking shoes at Wilson's Shoe Store. I think this pair will also last a long time."

1. Suppose that the last three pairs of hiking shoes were a different make than the ones you are buying now.

   strengthens ☐   *weakens* ☐   *does nothing* ☐

2. Suppose that Wilson's Shoe Store was bought out by a larger company recently.

   strengthens ☐   *weakens* ☐   *does nothing* ☐

3. Suppose that the last three pairs of hiking shoes are the same brand and kind as the ones you just bought.

   strengthens ☐   *weakens* ☐   *does nothing* ☐

4. Suppose that the shoemakers' union was recently on strike.

   strengthens ☐   *weakens* ☐   *does nothing* ☐

5. Suppose that you just bought a new puppy who likes to chew shoes.

   strengthens ☐   *weakens* ☐   *does nothing* ☐

6. Suppose that Toledo is not the capital of Ohio.

   strengthens ☐   *weakens* ☐   *does nothing* ☐

7. Suppose that the last three pairs of shoes were made by Nike, and these new shoes were also made by Nike.

   strengthens ☐   *weakens* ☐   *does nothing* ☐

8. Suppose you had the flu when you went into the shoe store and only *thought* you went into Wilson's.

   strengthens ☐   *weakens* ☐   *does nothing* ☐

   The three dogs you owned over the last ten years were German Shepherd dogs. All three of them were very well-behaved, and you were happy with them. Now you have just bought another German Shepherd puppy. You think it will be a nice dog as well.

9. Suppose that the last three dogs were females, and this one is also a female.

   strengthens ☐   *weakens* ☐   *does nothing* ☐

10. Suppose that the last three dogs were females, and this one is a male.

   strengthens ☐   *weakens* ☐   *does nothing* ☐

11. Suppose that the last three dogs were bought from a different kennel than this new one.

   strengthens ☐   *weakens* ☐   *does nothing* ☐

12. Suppose that the last three dogs you owned died before they were three years old.

   strengthens ☐   *weakens* ☐   *does nothing* ☐

13. Suppose that you owned the last three dogs when you were very young.

   strengthens ☐   *weakens* ☐   *does nothing* ☐

14. Suppose that your aunt Martha likes cats better than dogs.

   strengthens ☐   *weakens* ☐   *does nothing* ☐

15. Suppose that you hate small dogs.

   strengthens ☐   *weakens* ☐   *does nothing* ☐

16. Suppose that the new dog was trained as an attack dog, while the other three were not.

   strengthens ☐   *weakens* ☐   *does nothing* ☐

B. Decide whether the following analogies are, in your opinion, strong or weak.

17. "Chicago and Detroit are cities of approximately the same size. They are both located in the Midwest near a large body of water. I know Chicago has a bad crime problem, so Detroit must also have a bad crime problem."

strong ☐   *weak* ☐

18. "Rock music is bad for you. I heard a test was done with cows. They had two cows listen to music. One listened to Mozart, and the other listened to heavy metal. The one that listened to Mozart produced more milk and acted more contented, while the one that listened to heavy metal ate more, knocked over the milk bucket, and grew a horn."

strong ☐   *weak* ☐

19. "*David Copperfield* is a novel by Charles Dickens, set in England, and I hated it. *Oliver Twist* is a novel by Charles Dickens, set in England, and I hated it. *Great Expectations* is a novel by Charles Dickens, set in England. I think I will hate it."

strong ☐   *weak* ☐

20. "Since a single human cell becomes a grown man over a period of a few years, then surely it can't be impossible for a single-cell organism to become the human race over a period of several million years."

strong ☐   *weak* ☐

21. BERT: You shouldn't put saccharin in your coffee – it's bad for you. Saccharin has been known to cause cancer in lab rats.

strong ☐   *weak* ☐

22. "I liked *It's a Wonderful Life*, and that movie had James Stewart in it. I liked *Flight of the Phoenix*, and that movie had James Stewart in it. I

liked *Mr. Smith Goes to Washington,* and that movie had James Stewart in it. This next movie has James Stewart in it. I think I will like it."

strong ☐   weak ☐

23. "Humor can be dissected, as a frog can, but the thing dies in the process." – E. B. White

strong ☐   weak ☐

24. "Noise proves nothing. Often a hen who has merely laid an egg cackles as if she had laid an asteroid." – Mark Twain

strong ☐   weak ☐

25. "The progress of humanity is like climbing an endless ladder; it is impossible to climb higher without first taking the lower steps.... Hence it is no accident that the first cultures arose in places where the Aryan, in his encounters with lower peoples, subjugated them and bent them to his will. They then became the first technical instrument in the service of a developing culture." – Adolf Hitler, *Mein Kampf*

strong ☐   weak ☐

C. Read the following examples and answer the questions listed below them.

"Legal rights for mosquitoes! New studies show that mosquitoes have a similar genetic makeup to lawyers. Yes, a study conducted by the American Lawyer Behavior Research Trust (ALBRT) finds that there are striking similarities between mosquitoes and the common lawyer. And, yes, you've probably already guessed what they are. It seems mosquitoes have been found to have an obnoxious propensity towards the sucking of human blood, a behavioral trait formerly thought to be found only in leeches and lawyers. Mosquitoes have also been known to carry viruses and bacteria from host to host, thus contributing to the spread of disease, an ability long attributed to lawyers who propagate and multiply, leading to a weak and diseased society. 'We believe that mosquitoes are the closest living ancestors to the modern lawyer…and the differences are very minor,' says Harry Johnson, Vice President of the American Lawyer Behavior Research Trust. 'Since lawyers are allowed to practice law, we think mosquitoes should not be barred from taking the bar exams either.' 'While mosquitoes share approximately 75 percent of their genetic makeup with lawyers,' he says, 'the reason we put mosquitoes earlier on the geologic column is because they are not as developed as lawyers. Mosquitoes aren't able to get blood out of a turnip,' he states. 'We are currently searching for the missing link between mosquitoes and lawyers.'"

26. What is being compared here?

27. How does this show that the similarities between mosquitoes and lawyers are major and the differences minor?

28. What conclusion is drawn from this analogy?

29. In your opinion, is this conclusion justified?

yes   no

"The Great Ape Legal Project (GALP) is a joint project of the Animal Legal Defense Fund and the Great Ape Project International. Its goal is to establish legal rights for nonhuman great apes, including the right to life, liberty, and protection from torture....

'...We now have sufficient information about the capacities of great apes to make it clear that the moral boundary we draw between us and them is indefensible,' states Peter Singer, who cofounded the Great Ape Project in 1993. Research by Dr. Roger Fouts, Dr. Jane Goodall, and other primatologists has demonstrated that chimpanzees are aware, that they experience pain, and have rich mental and social lives. As individuals they are highly intelligent and have

well-developed cognitive skills. They express a broad range of emotions previ-
ously thought to be limited to humans – joy, sadness, grief, rage, fear, and even
a sense of humor. They can reason, plan for the future, make and use tools, be
curious and inventive, engage in sophisticated nonverbal communications, and
learn over three hundred signs in American Sign Language. Chimpanzees are
our closest biological relatives, sharing 98.4 percent of our DNA…Because the
similarities between us are so compelling, there is no ethical justification for
the difference in legal status." – Animal Legal Defense Fund

30. What is being compared here?

31. How does this show that the similarities between humans and apes are
major and the differences minor?

32. What conclusion is drawn from this analogy?

33. In your opinion, is this conclusion justified?

　　　　　　yes　　　　　　　　　　　　　　　*no*

Lesson 26

Post Hoc Ergo Propter Hoc

Post hoc ergo propter hoc is a Latin phrase which means "after this, therefore because of this." Apparently, this name was given to this fallacy back when Latin was popular among fallacy detectives. The name has stuck, so we aren't changing it now.

> ***Post hoc ergo propter hoc* is concluding that since A happened before B, A must have caused B.**

Suppose you live in Illinois, and it is the middle of February. As usual, it is thirty-two degrees below zero with six and a half feet of snow. You hate cold weather and wish it was warmer, so you turn on the weather report on television. The weatherman says, "Tomorrow the temperature will rise up to a blistering thirty-three degrees." The next day, this does happen. The top quarter-inch of snow melts.

"Whoa," you gasp. "That weatherman is some guy. He says it will get warmer, and then it does. The weatherman must have made it warmer." Quickly, you call up the station and ask the weatherman to make it sunny with highs of seventy-eight and lows of seventy-two for the next week.

Illustration by Tim Hodge.

You have committed the fallacy of *post hoc ergo propter hoc*. You assumed that since the weatherman said it would get warmer before it got warmer, the weatherman caused it to get warmer.

> Three months ago, we were all doing fine – the budget was balanced, the economy was great, we were at peace with other nations, and the weather was warm. Then we elected a new president. Since then everything has gone down-hill. Now we have a large budget deficit, the economy is in the pits, we're at war with Antarctica, and it's cold outside. It's obvious that the new president caused all this because he was elected just before all this happened.

If the new president was elected just before everything went bad, that doesn't necessarily mean the new president caused it to go bad. This is a common error in reasoning. We see something happen, good or bad, then look for what happened just before it – expecting to find the cause. But what happened just before it is often not the cause.

If we trip and sprain an ankle, we will think of all the "unlucky" things that happened that day – we saw a black cat, walked under a ladder, or opened an umbrella in the house. We superstitiously conclude that these unrelated things caused the sprained ankle because they happened before it.

> FATHER: Son, I think this electric guitar you bought is influencing you for the worse.
> SON: Uh, why, dude…er…Dad?
> FATHER: Ever since you bought it, you have been growing your hair longer and have been slouching around the house with your hands in your pockets. We have also noticed that you have spoken more disrespectfully to your mother and me, and you haven't been doing as much housework.

This father is committing the *post hoc ergo propter hoc* fallacy. He concludes that since the electric guitar was bought just before the bad behavior began, the electric guitar caused the bad behavior. While the electric guitar may be causing the bad behavior, it is also possible that a general decline in his son's morals is causing the buying of the electric guitar, slouching, disrespectfulness, and laziness.

Sometimes a *post hoc ergo propter hoc* is true – what happened before *is* the cause. When an egg breaks on a concrete floor, it seems logical to think immediately of what you did just before it broke – you dropped it, so that was the cause. However, if A happened before B, we don't have enough reason to conclude immediately that A caused B – we need to find out a bit more.

Exercises

A. For these examples of *post hoc ergo propter hoc*, give some other, possibly overlooked, causes for the events in question.

1. "I've been looking into the history of wars. It seems as if just before any war, all the countries involved build large armies. I think building a large army causes war."

2. "These shoes are my best shoes. They help me to pass tests. The last three times I wore them was on test days, and I passed the tests."

B. Name the faulty reasoning, if any, in the following examples.

3. "Religion is a waste of time and energy because there's no reason to spend our lives in prayer when we all have better things to do."

4. "Yesterday I was painting a room. I was up on a ladder when I decided it needed to be moved. When I climbed down, I wasn't thinking about what I was doing and walked under the ladder. Just when I realized this was unlucky, I tripped over a black cat which was under the ladder, then fell over and smashed the mirror which I was about to install. Now do you understand why I have two broken legs and my house was repossessed?"

5. PERSON IN POST OFFICE: The United States is the most powerful nation today, and you work for the powerful U.S. government as a mailman here in the Wichiwachi Post Office. So, don't tell me you don't know where my package went to – all the forces of western civilization are arrayed on your side!

6. "Communist governments always end in failure. Look what happened to the Soviet Union."

7. MRS.: My head hurts. I think these pills are giving me headaches.
   MR.: Why do you think that, honey?
   MRS.: Because it says "may cause headaches" right here on the bottle.

8. "A cloud is 90 percent water; a watermelon is 90 percent water. Therefore, since a plane can fly through a cloud, a plane can fly through a watermelon."

9. "Ever since Clyde started cozying up with the teacher and talking really nice to her, he has been getting A's and B's on his tests in her class. It's very obvious that he is now the teacher's pet. I think it's unfair."

10. YOUNG BACHELOR: Either I marry her and she drives me crazy with all her talking, or I don't marry her and I go crazy the rest of my life thinking about her.

11. JENNY: Meat is very bad for you. You should never eat it. It rots in your stomach.

BERT: How do you know that?

JENNY: Well, it takes over twenty-four hours to digest meat. Why don't you just take a piece of bacon and set it out in the driveway for twenty-four hours and see what it smells like afterward? Yuck!

12. POLITICAL CANDIDATE A: I think the federal government has no business in education.

POLITICAL CANDIDATE B: So you don't think education is a national priority then?

13. FARMER MCDONALD: Ever since they put up that new power plant across the river, we haven't had a bit of rain. I'm tellin' you, mankind has gotten too big for its britches when it fiddles around with nature.

14. Larry was a kind, gentle man. He always spoke softly and was kind to his wife. Then his wife started to buy crunchy instead of creamy peanut butter. Soon, Larry showed signs of being easily irritated. His voice sounded gruff, and he was rude to the neighbors. When Larry's wife noticed this, she went around the house and threw out all of the crunchy peanut butter.

15. BERT: I want to learn how to ski. I know a guy who lives in Vermont and he skis all the time, and he says it's the best.

CLYDE: Naw, you want to do snowboarding. Its the best. I know a guy who lives in Colorado and he snowboards and says it's way better than skiing. My friend is right 'cause the mountains in Colorado are way bigger than the ones in Vermont.

16. ELDER AND WISER BROTHER: Some congressman pled the Fifth in court today. Have you learned what they mean by "pled the Fifth?"
LITTLE SISTER: I think it means the Fifth Amendment to the Constitution.
ELDER AND WISER BROTHER: And what is the Fifth Amendment about?
LITTLE SISTER: Temporary insanity?

17. "If you think we are too secluded in this town, why don't you go commit a crime and go to prison? I'll bet you meet some pretty varied people in there."

18. MOTHER: There you go making the candlesticks on the mantle symmetrical. You're becoming obsessive compulsive!
DAUGHTER: I'm just straightening them a little.
MOTHER: Before you know it, you'll be complaining when someone steps on the carpet and makes footprints.
DAUGHTER: No, I won't.
MOTHER: And then you'll start washing your hands every few minutes, and refuse to touch doorknobs.

19. JENNY: You can't just steal that!
SHOPLIFTER: Why not? They do it in baseball all the time.

Lesson 27

Post Hoc Ergo Propter Hoc in Statistics

We have all heard people tell us:

> Young man, you want to make plenty of money when you grow up, don't you?
> Well, you need to attend the best college you can afford. Studies have shown
> that the better the college you go to, the more money you make later in life.
> – Concerned Friend

Your concerned friend is only thinking of your future happiness. He thinks going to a good college will make you richer. He thinks his advice is backed up with hard, cold evidence – and it is. It's only the interpretation he gets all wrong.

Your concerned friend has probably seen a study similar to this one:

A prominent college – let's call it Stonehenge College – will look up all the people who graduated about twenty years before and survey them – how much money they are making, what kind of jobs they have, etc. The results confirm what they thought. The average Stonehenge graduate makes $75,000 a year and has a condo in Palm Beach. They will then compare this with the numbers from similar studies done by less prominent colleges, and bang! Stonehenge graduates make more money.

> "I can't argue with the numbers," you say.
> "Then you can't argue with the conclusion," they say. "Attending Stonehenge
> College will make you a rich person! Right?"

Wrong. Enter *post hoc ergo propter hoc*. If the average Stonehenge graduate makes more money *after* attending Stonehenge, that doesn't mean he is making more money *because* he attended Stonehenge. And, incidentally, if *you* attend Stonehenge, *you* aren't necessarily going to be rich either.

"Then how do you explain these hard cold facts? Why do Stonehenge graduates make more money if it isn't because they went to Stonehenge?" they ask.

It is true that having a Stonehenge diploma may automatically get you a high-paying job. However, if Stonehenge College is as highly ranked as it claims to be, it would probably be difficult to get into unless you are both smart and motivated. So the real cause for these Stonehenge graduates making a lot of money is not that they went to Stonehenge College but the fact that they are smart and motivated.

A and B don't have to actually follow each other in time to be a *post hoc ergo propter hoc* – they can both happen at the same time. This fallacy is also being committed when somebody says that since A and B are commonly seen together, one must have caused the other.

> A recent study by the New England Association of Connection Concoct-
> ers finds that there is a great difference in test scores between people who
> listen to classical music and people who listen to more popular music. People
> who normally listen to at least fifteen minutes of classical music a day scored
> many points higher on standardized tests than people who normally listened
> to heavy metal. Those who listened to country music scored the lowest. The
> report says, "These results have far-reaching ramifications for our everyday
> life. Music has a far greater power on our basic functions than we ever thought."
> – something Hans made up

Look out for their "obvious" conclusion: if you want to score higher on a test, break out the Mozart. And, to carry it a step further, heavy metal music makes you dumb. If classical music and good grades are seen together, then the classical music must have *caused* the good grades. We all want this to be true – it even seems logical. But why couldn't it be the other way around? The people who do well on tests are smarter and tend to have a better taste in music and listen to classical, and those who tend to do worse on tests listen to heavy metal and country.

> Does failing to brush your teeth encourage you to murder? A recent study,
> conducted over the past fifty years, has revealed a relationship between tooth-
> brush sales and crime rates. Whenever toothbrush sales in the United States
> drop, the crime rate climbs. Also, when people start to buy more toothbrushes,

there are fewer crimes.

"This is astounding," says the president of Colgate. "We have always recommended that people brush their teeth, but we never thought it was this important."– another thing Hans made up

People draw wild connections between things which would normally appear to be totally unrelated. This example could be a case where an overlooked cause is behind both things. The economy takes a dive and people don't have enough money to buy new toothbrushes. And people turn to crime because their businesses aren't doing too well – also a result of the bad economy.

Illustration by Rob Corley.

That's why our product is so important!

Exercises

A. What form of faulty reasoning, if any, is being used in the following examples?

1. JENNY: You know jaywalking is against the law, don't you?
   BERT: And I suppose you never jaywalked in your life?

2. "I heard Candidate Schwartz say that he wasn't a Democrat, so he must be running on the Republican ticket."

3. MR.: I've changed my mind. I've decided not to marry you.
   MISS: But we've been planning on getting married all afternoon.
   MR.: Well, I know, but I heard most suicides are committed in June. We all know that most weddings are in June. Marriage must drive guys to suicide. I don't want to get depressed and kill myself.

4. MR.: Well, maybe I will marry you.
   MISS: What! Why are you changing your mind again?
   MR.: I heard somewhere else that married people live longer than unmarried people. I don't want to die young.
   MISS: That's it. Just forget the whole thing. I'm not going to marry such a fickle guy. All you care about is yourself.

5. "Studies have shown that people who exercise several times a week have a lower chance of heart disease. You should exercise. It certainly won't do you any harm, and it might do you some good."

6. JENNY: I think I'm going to become a vegetarian. It will make me healthier.
   BERT: Why? How do you know it will make you healthier?
   JENNY: Because I read somewhere that vegetarians are healthier than the average American.

7. GOVERNMENT REPORT: A low-income level seems to be the greatest factor contributing to why some families where both parents work full-time are still below the poverty line.

8. "A few years ago, they raised the speed limit in this state to seventy-five miles per hour, and now we have a higher accident rate. I think the higher speed limit is causing more accidents – if people are driving faster, they can't control their vehicles as well, and this results in more accidents."

9. "Babe Ruth always used Louisville Sluggers whenever he went up to bat. He said they were the best bats around. All the New York Yankees used them, in fact. I think I'll buy one."

10. "Our rooster crows every morning. Then the sun comes up. Now do you understand how important roosters are?"

11. "I have argued with my pastor three times in the last month. Each time, he gets angry, and those little veins in his forehead stick out. Therefore,

anytime anybody argues with him, he will get angry and those little veins will stick out."

12. CHILD: Who made God?

13. FATHER: What is that? You have a tattoo!
SON: Ah, Dad, it's only a turtle.
FATHER: Don't you know that all the people in prison have tattoos? I don't want you to end up there.

14. "Sleeping for too long is bad for your health. Researchers have found that those who sleep for longer than seven hours a night have a much higher death rate. This six-year study analyzed the sleeping patterns of over a million adults who were over thirty years old. These researchers found that those who slept eight hours a night were 12 percent more likely to die within six years. Those who slept five hours a night lived longer than those who slept more than eight hours."

15. "Why are you punishing me, Mom? I'm your kid. Isn't blood thicker than water?"

Lesson 28

Proof by Lack of Evidence

The *proof by lack of evidence* fallacy is claiming something is true simply because nobody has yet given any evidence to the contrary.

> MASTER TORTURER: Confess! It was you who said the king looked like a platypus.
>
> ACCUSED: No!
>
> MASTER TORTURER: All right, Tony, start tickling him.
>
> ACCUSED: No! Hehe…I…hehehe…didn't…hehe…say…hehe…it…hehe…gasp!
>
> MASTER TORTURER: But you must have said it. You haven't yet given us any proof that you didn't say it.… Tickle him some more, Tony.

This torturer's reasoning is wrong. How could the accused give the torturer any evidence that he *didn't* say something?

When someone makes an assertion – "you are guilty of this crime" – that person is the one who is obliged to back it up with evidence – "you are guilty of this crime because I saw you do it." Saying "you are guilty because you haven't shown me you aren't" would be very lazy reasoning. It shifts the burden of proof onto the accused, when the accuser should have the burden of proving his accusation.

The person who makes an assertion is the one who must prove it. Let's take a look at an assertion.

> BERT: There are mountain lions living in Illinois.

This assertion needs to be backed up with evidence.

BERT: I think there are mountain lions living in Illinois.
JENNY: Yeah, right. Prove it.
BERT: Just look behind you.
JENNY: Heeeeelllllllp!

This evidence is good. However, suppose Bert said:

BERT: There must be mountain lions living in Illinois because I haven't seen any proof that there aren't any.

This would be committing the proof by lack of evidence fallacy. He can't claim that mountain lions live in Illinois only because there isn't any evidence to the contrary. This fallacy works the same for the opposite assertion.

JENNY: There are no mountain lions living in Illinois.
BERT: How do you know that?
JENNY: Well, prove to me there are some.

This is also the proof by lack of evidence fallacy. Just because no one has seen any mountain lions in Illinois, that doesn't mean we can say for sure there are none – they may hide very well. Jenny is the one who needs to prove what she claims.

JENNY: There are no mountain lions in Illinois because I have just examined every square inch of Illinois simultaneously, and there were none.

Examining every inch of Illinois simultaneously would be difficult – but it would do the trick.

People make some very imaginative claims using the proof by lack of evidence fallacy.

TOUR GUIDE: And now I will show you the famous statue called *The Thinker*. Legend has it that at night *The Thinker* comes down from his post and walks around the city. But nobody ever sees him. He's so fast he can run back to his post quicker than the blink of an eye.

NOT-SO-GULLIBLE TOURIST: Ha! That's the most ridiculous bunch of baloney I've ever heard. How could you prove that?

TOUR GUIDE: But, sir, how do you know it *isn't* true?

Since there is no real way to prove this claim is true, the tour guide must use the proof by lack of evidence fallacy.

DILBERT reprinted by permission of United Feature Syndicate, Inc.

Proof by lack of evidence

Not Proof by Lack of Evidence

In a court of criminal law, the burden of proof is always on the accuser – the one who says "that person committed a crime." The accuser can never say, "That man is guilty because he can't prove he didn't do it." Unfortunately, in many courtrooms of the past, innocent people were punished because this was allowed – just like our first example. But in a courtroom today, an accused person is assumed innocent until proven guilty. In a courtroom, an accused person can rightfully say, "I am innocent because you can't prove me guilty." This is not the proof by lack of evidence fallacy because, in a courtroom, the burden of proof is always on the accuser.

Exercises

A. Which attorney is committing the proof by lack of evidence fallacy?

1. PROSECUTING ATTORNEY: The defense in this case has not given one shred of evidence that the accused was not at the scene of the crime at the time of the murder. They have not given one shred of evidence that

the accused is not a homicidal maniac. They have not given one shred of evidence that the accused was not strong enough to kill the victim. In the light of these facts, how can you, the jury, acquit this man?"

DEFENSE ATTORNEY: The prosecution in this case has not presented to us any proof that my client was at the scene of the crime at the time of the murder. They have not shown us that my client had any murderous intentions. They have not even shown that my client had enough strength to commit the crime. I must insist that my client is innocent.

prosecuting　　　　　　　*defense attorney*
attorney

B. What form of faulty reasoning, if any, is used in the following examples?

2. TORTURER: You are a spy. You can't prove that you aren't one, so you are a spy. Confess, or we will stretch your body out until you are a foot taller.
   ACCUSED: Ha, you did it – you committed a fallacy! I learned all about it in a book called *The Fallacy Detective*.
   TORTURER: That's enough cheek out of you. Brutus, give the wheel another turn.

3. "The Ford Zip automobile is the safest car to drive. An independent test laboratory placed two hundred three-toed tree frogs in two hundred Ford Zips, then crashed the cars. Every single frog lived through the crashes and, in fact, seemed to act happier afterward."

4. "The reports of my death are greatly exaggerated." – Mark Twain

5. "My friend John is insane. He doesn't look like it, but he's madder than a March hare. He may look perfectly normal on the outside, but you never know when he'll up and do something crazy. Yep, deep down, he's

a raving lunatic. Now, you may ask, how do I know this? Well, can you prove to me that he is sane? I'll bet you can't."

6. INTERVIEWER: What do you think should be done about people who swear in public?
   MAN ON STREET: I think it should be against the law.
   INTERVIEWER: Oh, I suppose you're against the right to free speech, then?

7. "I've visited France, and I know that the French are a very sophisticated and artistic people. That's why I trust that you, Mr. Arnot, will be able to design my granddaughter's birthday cake as a perfection of culinary delight."

8. SON TO FATHER: Dad, a family is like a nation in many ways. They both are a group of people related to each other in some way, and they both are an independent entity. Since we all know that a nation works best when it is a democracy, I think we should hold an election to see who will make the decisions around here.

9. "The *Illiad* tells the story of Troy, but archeologists have not found any evidence that the city of Troy existed. Therefore, the city of Troy never existed, and the *Illiad* is all fiction and untrue."

10. POLITICIAN: My fellow voters, I know you are either among the arrogant rich, the lazy poor, or one of the contented middle class like me.

11. ADVERTISEMENT: You can buy the new Sensitivity perfume, or you can smell bad all day.

12. PATIENT: Doctor, I've been having these urges to go out and rob a bank lately. Should I be worried about this?

    S. FREUD: I don't think so. You see these urges come from your evolutionary past. The survival of the fittest dictates that we try to gain an advantage over other life forms by destroying their means of living. Robbing the bank destroys other people's means of living and helps you to survive. Your desires are just outworkings of the epic struggle for survival.

13. "America is on the brink of an economic depression. Pretty soon all the businesses that we think are stable will go bankrupt. We have hard times ahead of us. I see no way around it. After all, how can you show me that things are going to continue to be as hunky-dory as they have been forever? You can't."

14. "There can be nothing wrong with price-fixing. I am sure everybody will agree that a store clerk has the right to fix the prices as he chooses."

15. "Christianity came along in the first century, and a few hundred years after that, the Roman Empire fell. Christianity must have made it fall."

16. "There's no point in listening to you. Everybody knows you're just a little do-gooder."

17. CLYDE: Maybe the Jewish Holocaust was okay?
JENNY: That is terrible! You think it was all right for the Nazis to try to exterminate the Jews?
CLYDE: Maybe. If the Nazi leaders proposed it, and all the German people approved of it and carried it out, I can't see how they could all have been misguided.

18. "My brother sucked on his thumb until he was ten years old, and now he is a serial killer. Never let your children suck their thumbs!"

19. FARMER MCDONALD: I've been lookin' at them rich farmers. I've been tryin' to find out what makes 'em rich.
FARMER BROWN: What did you find out?
FARMER MCDONALD: Every one of them rich farmers has a brand new John Deere tractor. I think that is what makes 'em rich. I'm gonna buy myself one of them John Deere tractors.

20. A recent study has linked the current civil war in Angola with rainfall in the fertile valleys of California. Ever since the civil war in Angola broke out, California has had only small amounts of rainfall. "This is terrible. I don't have half the crop I had ten years ago," says Hank Junior, a kiwi farmer in central California. "Somebody needs to go to Africa and tell those people that their actions affect more people than they think."

21. "There is a God. Nobody has ever come up with any conclusive evidence that there isn't one."

22. FARMER MCDONALD: I just returned from my visit to California. Boy, they sure have some high mountains over there. One was over fourteen thousand feet high.

23. In another recent study, researchers have discovered an astounding fact. Auto accidents tend to rise when people eat more cabbage. Yes, that's right. Researchers have been studying the connection between the consumption of cabbage for people over eighteen and their driving history. "It seems, when people eat more cabbage, they are more often in motor accidents, and when they eat less cabbage, they are in fewer accidents," says one researcher. "These are intriguing results. We don't know what to do with them."

24. "I like The Black Dogs because they're my favorite band."

25. SENATOR: I don't think we need to talk to the people in the Justice Department about the practicality of enforcing this bill. The Justice Department is full of Republicans, so they are already biased against it.

Propaganda

Lesson 29

What Is Propaganda?

Advertisers are always looking for ways to pressure us to buy their products. Manufacturers design everything from automobiles to bars of soap in ways which make them appear irresistible.

"Buy Swiss Springtime soap – it makes you feel all clean and fresh!"

Manufacturers make their automobiles look more tough, more luxurious, or more trendy – all to make us want to buy them.

"BMW: the ultimate driving machine."

In the court room, lawyers give the jury more and more reasons to side with them in the case.

"This criminal is so low that he would steal from his own mother!"

These are all examples of propaganda.

Propaganda is any strategy for spreading our beliefs or ideas.

Propaganda can be found in a political speech, a television show, an advertisement, and many other places. Propagandists use many different methods to spread their ideas. We call these propaganda techniques.

Propaganda is not always bad. There is nothing necessarily wrong with spreading our ideas and encouraging people to buy our product – as long as we do it honestly. Unfortunately, sometimes the reasons people give us to buy their product, vote for their candidate, or do what they want aren't very good.

188

A truck dealer will pressure us to buy his truck because it looks tougher – not because it necessarily is tougher. The lawyer in the courtroom will pressure the jury to feel that his side is the right one – not to know that his side is the right one.

PEANUTS reprinted by permission of United Feature Syndicate, Inc.

***Manipulative propaganda* is used when someone plays with our emotions in a way designed to make us agree with them without thinking through the matter carefully.**

In this chapter, when we discuss propaganda, we mean manipulative propaganda.

When two different propagandists manipulate our emotions in different ways, we often can't decide which emotion to follow.

> DEFENSE ATTORNEY: Ladies and gentlemen of the jury, I urge you to acquit John Jones of this crime of murder. He is married and has three children. If he is executed or goes to prison for life, his family will end up in the poorhouse.
>
> PROSECUTING ATTORNEY: Ladies and gentlemen of the jury, I urge you to convict John Jones of this crime of murder. We need to put him where he can never commit any more crimes. If you don't convict him, you may be his next victim.

Notice how both these arguments sound very convincing when you first look at them? The only problem is, you can't take both sides – one side, at least, must be wrong.

Two propaganda techniques are used in this example. The defense attorney wants the jury to side with him out of pity, and the prosecuting attorney wants the jury to side with him out of fear.

Neither attorney addresses the real issue – the issue that the jury is supposed to decide: whether John Jones actually committed the murder.

Manipulative propaganda is like a red herring fallacy: it avoids the important issues that should be addressed; it distracts us.

When we think we are being manipulated by propaganda, it is useful to ask ourselves: is this person actually proving what he is saying? Or is he merely giving me the impression that he has proven it to me? Is what he is saying relevant?

This chapter gives you tools and names to make you more aware of the emotions in advertisements and political speeches. We want you to make better decisions when you buy something or vote for somebody.

Illustration by Rob Corley.

Exercises

A. Answer the following questions.

1. What kinds of people use propaganda?

2. Do only bad people use propaganda?

3. What are some places where we hear propaganda?

4. Is it always wrong to use propaganda?

5. Are the viewpoints of propagandists always wrong?

6. Is propaganda always manipulative?

7. Does propaganda always play on our emotions?

8. Is propaganda always irrelevant?

9. Does propaganda always lie?

10. What is the capital of Australia?

B. Which of the following advertisements are using manipulative and emotional propaganda techniques?

11. "There is a God! The majority of Americans believe there is some kind of divine being!"

    manipulative ☐   *not manipulative* ☐

12. "Real hard-working, moral people believe God exists."

    manipulative ☐   *not manipulative* ☐

13. "Only underdeveloped people believe in a God. Religion is only an evolutionary hangover."

    manipulative ☐   *not manipulative* ☐

14. "God does not exist because I can prove it!"

    manipulative ☐   *not manipulative* ☐

15. "Wouldn't you feel bad if you believed all your life that there was a God, and then you found out when you died that there wasn't one?"

    manipulative ☐   *not manipulative* ☐

16. PASTOR, HITTING PULPIT WITH BIBLE: There is a God!…Thump!…There is a God!…Thump, thump!…There is a God! Thump, thump, thump!…There is a God!…Thump, thump, thump, thump!

    manipulative ☐   *not manipulative* ☐

Lesson 30

Appeal to Fear

Appeal to fear **is a propaganda technique.** *Appeal to fear* **is used when someone makes you fear the consequences of not doing what he wants.**

Let's go back to the example we gave in the last lesson:

PROSECUTING ATTORNEY: Ladies and gentlemen of the jury, I urge you to convict John Jones of this crime of murder. We need to put him where he can never commit any more crimes. If you don't convict him, you may be his next victim.

This statement does not address the proper question: did John Jones actually commit this murder? Instead, the prosecuting attorney is trying to disturb the jury with the fear of being murdered. "I need to convict this man whether he is guilty or not; I may be his next victim!" This reasoning, of course, is illogical.

It is never good to act out of fear. However, fear is a strong motivator. When people fear something, they tend to not think matters through. They think out of cringe-reflex. "Help! Something bad could happen!"

Appeal to fear is used in commercials like this one:

ADVERTISEMENT: A picture of a dingy bathroom. "Is this what your bathroom looks like?" This is followed by a microscopic close-up of the bathtub, showing little bugs crawling around. "Here is what is going on where you can't see. Use Everclean for a fresher-looking bathroom."

This advertisement wants us to dread the thought of little bugs crawling around in our bathrooms (whether or not they do any real damage) and then,

193

hopefully, buy their product.

When the person appealing to fear is actually the one dealing out the fear, the situation can take on a more brutal form.

> RESTAURANT OWNER: You no lika da pizzas? I send over my cousin Tony for a little change a' mind. He maka you lika da pizzas.

This can be very effective. When someone fears something or someone, he often makes decisions which he might not make in calmer situations. If big-fisted Tony is across from us, we might think it wiser to decide we like the pizza after all – no matter how many anchovies are on it.

> "The Nazis used to send the following notice to German readers who let their subscriptions lapse: 'Our paper certainly deserves the support of every German. We shall continue to forward copies of it to you and hope that you will not want to expose yourself to unfortunate consequences in the case of cancellation.'" – *Parade Magazine*, May 9, 1971

This style of persuasion can be very effective. We would want to renew our subscriptions, even if we didn't like the paper.

PEANUTS reprinted by permission of United Feature Syndicate, Inc.

Linus is persuaded by an appeal to fear.

Not an Appeal to Fear

An appeal to fear is not being used when somebody threatens us but doesn't try to change our opinion.

> BANK ROBBER: If you don't transfer all of the money into my account, I will

give you a bad case of lead poisoning with this gun here.

This is not an appeal to fear because the robber is not trying to change our minds; he is just giving us our options – do what he says or die. Of course, sometimes there is a fine line between an appeal to fear and a mere threat. But for us, an appeal to fear is trying to change someone's opinion out of fear of something. A threat is just offering someone a choice between doing what we want or suffering the consequences.

Exercises

Which of the following examples are an appeal to fear?

1. ADVERTISEMENT FOR A NEW CAR WITH IMPROVED BRAKES: Scene of a mother driving the new car with young daughter sleeping in the passenger seat. Suddenly, a deer jumps in front of the car. The screen freezes. "Does your car have all-wheel drive?"

   appeal to fear ☐   *not appeal to fear* ☐

2. "Chevy Suburban. Like a rock."

   appeal to fear ☐   *not appeal to fear* ☐

3. "Do you know what kind of damage a loose cow can do on your farm? Imagine what would happen if your electric fence failed and your cows wandered into the neighbor's field. Buy a Zapper electric fence, and you won't have to worry about it."

   appeal to fear ☐   *not appeal to fear* ☐

4. C.E.O.: Before we begin this board meeting – where we will be deciding some important things – I would like to remind you who is the boss and who can fire you.

appeal to fear ☐   *not appeal to fear* ☐

5. PARENT: I hope you agree with me that my little Johnny did well on that last test – I contribute a lot of money to this school.

appeal to fear ☐   *not appeal to fear* ☐

6. "Everybody put your money in this bag, or my cousin Vern, over here, will sing 'The Star-Spangled Banner' really loudly!"

appeal to fear ☐   *not appeal to fear* ☐

7. "Mothers of River City, heed that warning before it's too late. Watch for the telltale signs of corruption [from the pool table]: the minute your son leaves the house, does he rebuckle his knickerbockers below the knee? Is there a nicotine stain on his index finger? A dime novel hidden in the corncrib? Is he startin' to memorize jokes from *Cap'n Billie's Whizbang*? Are certain words creeping into his conversation? Words like: 'swell' and 'so's your ole man.' Well, if so my friends, you got trouble." – Professor Harold Hill in *The Music Man*

appeal to fear ☐   *not appeal to fear* ☐

8. "Disperse, you rebels!"

appeal to fear ☐   *not appeal to fear* ☐

9. "Disperse, you rebels, or we will fire!"

   appeal to fear   ☐   *not appeal to fear*   ☐

10. "I hope you see the reasonableness of dispersing – remember who has the most guns."

   appeal to fear   ☐   *not appeal to fear*   ☐

Lesson 31

Appeal to Pity

When someone tries to make us do something only because we pity him or we pity something associated with him, he is using the propaganda technique called *appeal to pity*.

RADIO ADVERTISEMENT: Mr. Jones lost the last election because his opponent used a smear campaign to discredit him. Mr. Jones lost the election before that because of voter fraud. Mr. Jones lost the election before that because nobody knew who he was. Don't you think it is about time you voted for Mr. Jones?

Poor Mr. Jones. But wait a minute – this advertisement doesn't give us any real reasons why Mr. Jones would make a good officeholder.

OFFICER: I stopped you because you were going fifty-eight miles per hour in a twenty-five-mile-per-hour zone. I'm going to have to write you a ticket.
MOTORIST: But officer, this is the fifth ticket I've gotten this year. If I get another ticket, then they will take my license away, and I won't be able to drive to work. My wife and children will starve.

The motorist may be in a predicament, but his point is irrelevant. The very fact that he has received five tickets in one year probably means he doesn't care enough about his family to drive safely. This motorist is attempting to manipulate the officer by appealing to his pity.

"After a debate touching on their own four-legged friends, senators [of the California senate] voted to forbid condominiums and mobile home parks from completely banning pets.

Supporters said the bill would help many Californians, including older residents, whose lives could be brightened by animals.

Arguing for the bill, Senate Leader John Burton, D-San Francisco, recalled that his own mother was greatly comforted by her little dog after Burton's father passed away.

'That poodle was a companion to my mother, who, naturally, after the death of my father, was living at home alone,' Burton said." – *The Sacramento Bee*, August 23, 2000

Does the story about John Burton's mother make you feel sad? But, did his mother live in a condominium? Does his anecdote show us that we need to make it illegal to ban pets in condominiums?

Sometimes an appeal to pity tries to make us feel guilty.

FLIER FROM THE APPALACHIAN CLUB: Every year, millions of people around the world build new homes and put groceries in bags made out of trees taken from the Amazon rain forests. It is estimated that twelve species of animal become extinct every 65.944 seconds. Don't you think you should do something about this?

Doesn't this appeal make you feel at least a little guilty? But wait a minute. This flyer does not show us how using a grocery bag will make animals become extinct.

PEANUTS reprinted by permission of United Feature Syndicate, Inc.

Appeal to pity

Exercises

What form of propaganda, if any, is being used?

1. CREDIT CARD ADVERTISEMENT: Picture of a shark attacking. "Free card replacement if lost, stolen, or devoured."

2. "Gun manufacturers should do something about all those guns we have lying around. My grandson was brutally murdered last summer by another child with a gun."

3. ADVERTISEMENT OF SHARP SPORTS SEDAN: It's friendly and loves to play.

4. "Teacher, please give me a passing grade. If I don't pass, my dad says I can't leave the house for a month."

5. "Could you please give me a little money? I am in trouble – my barn just burned down, I lost my job, my whole family has pneumonia, and the Mafia has a price on my head."

6. "Could you please give me a little money? I am in trouble – our house just burned down, the car was just repossessed, I lost my job, my whole

family has pneumonia, the Mafia has a price on my head, and I lost all my money to a robber."

7. PICTURE OF A LARGE EXPLOSION: Be careful on the 4th of July. People love you.

8. MRS.: I need a diamond ring.
   MR.: Why? You already have lots of jewelry.
   MRS.: Sniff, sniff, but, sniff, I just want to have something, sniff, to make me feel, sniff, better.

9. ADVERTISEMENT: Sweet and Smooth cigarettes

10. CRIMINAL: But judge, if you convict me, I'll be branded for life. When I get out, nobody will want me to work for them.

11. "Help! Our house is on fire, and my infant son is still inside. Can you please help us?"

12. ADVERTISEMENT: Should your kids have to worry about nuclear war?

Lesson 32

Bandwagon

When advertisements and articles encourage us to "join the millions," the propaganda technique of bandwagon is being used. We often want to do what "everybody else" is doing.

> CLYDE: Dad, can I go to see the movie *Attack of the Killer Wombats*?
> DAD: No, Son, you can't go. I heard that movie has violent scenes in it.
> CLYDE: Aw, come on. Everybody's going to see it.

Clyde is using the bandwagon technique on his dad.

The *bandwagon* technique invites us to jump on the bandwagon and do what everybody else is doing. This technique pressures us to do something just because many other people like us are doing it.

"More Americans get their news from ABC than from any other source."

Just because more Americans get their news from ABC, does that necessarily mean that ABC gives us the best news?

This propaganda technique is the reason why parents frequently ask their children:

> MOM: If (friend's name is inserted here) jumped off a cliff, would you?
> SON: Of course. Where's the cliff?

If all the other people in the world are doing something – like going to a particular movie, wearing a particular style of clothing, or believing a particular teaching – that isn't enough reason for us to do it also.

"This year, over 117,574 people will visit the Virgin Islands."

Bandwagon has a lot to do with peer pressure. We all have an urge to do what our friends are doing. Sometimes we know it is wrong, but we do it anyway.

The issue is not whether everybody else does it. The issue is whether it is right or wrong. Is that movie a good movie to see? Is this news source more reliable?

Illustration by Tim Hodge.

A bandwagon

Exercises

What form of propaganda, if any, is being used in the following examples?

1. CONSTITUENT STANDING IN FRONT OF SENATOR: Senator, I have walked all the way from Claremore, Oklahoma, barefoot, just to tell you not to vote for Senate bill 254.

2. MR.: I think we need to buy a new car.
   MRS.: Why? Our car is only a few years old, and we haven't had any problems with it yet.
   MR.: I think it is a good idea to buy a new car. It would make us look better to our neighbors. The Smiths just bought a new Cadillac, and the what's-their-names just bought a new Ford station wagon.

3. COMMENT ON AN INTERNET FORUM: Man, puppy52 has been posting on our forum forever. Everyone hates her. Then this new member joined, tinderbox, and she just starts ripping into puppy52. But tinderbox has never read a single post. She's just doing it because everybody else is.

4. PICTURE OF A MAN KNOCKING DOWN THE BERLIN WALL – THE MAN'S FIGURE IS SCRATCHED OUT: The greatest risk is in not taking one. AIG, world leaders in insurance and financial services.

5. MAN SEEN HOLDING SIGN ON STREET CORNER: Homeless and hungry.

6. MOM: If all your friends jumped off a cliff, would you?
   JOEY: Yes, where's the cliff?

7. "Join millions of Americans in the Freedom Club."

8. BERT: I heard that Greenland is applying to become the 51st state in the United States.
   CLYDE: I heard that too. Maybe it's true.

9. "Most Americans support the Equal Rights Amendment."

10. "I've just invented a perpetual motion machine which can run your car, power your house, and solve marital disputes all at once by just adding water. Unfortunately, the government is attempting to cover my discovery up because Exxon and Mobil would lose too much money, and now nobody believes me. Just send me $982 plus your firstborn son, and you can have one."

Lesson 33

Exigency

An exigency is an urgent need which demands immediate action. The *exigency* technique encourages us to "hurry up and agree, because we are running out of time."

Illustration by Rob Corley.

Hurry down, boys and girls!
This is my last porcupine!

This advertisement is motivating us to make up our minds and do what the speaker says before all the porcupines are gone. He wants us to buy them so quickly that we don't think about whether we really need a pet porcupine.

"Genuine lead teacups! Now 95 percent off! Hurry, while supplies last!"

Exigency **is being used when nothing more than a time limit is given as a reason for us to do what someone wants.**

> CALEB: Why don't you come to that movie with me?
>
> ISAAC: I don't think I should. My parents haven't seen it yet, and we don't know if it is any good.
>
> CALEB: But it's been playing at the theaters for several weeks, and if we wait anylonger, it might not be playing any longer.

In this example, Caleb isn't addressing the point which Isaac brought up (that his parents haven't seen it yet). Caleb is only talking about how the movie won't be playing for much longer.

Exercises

What form of propaganda, if any, is being used in the following examples?

1. "Boy, these things have been selling like hotcakes. Better hurry up and get one before they are all gone."

2. "How much do you love your Camry? Camry is America's favorite car for the fourth year in a row with more repeat buyers than any other car."

3. "Interest on a loan is at a really low rate right now – 1 percent. The last time it was this low it only stayed there for a few months, and then it went up really high. I encourage you to get a loan for a new house."

4. "Discover why thousands of people with low vision have purchased the VideoEye."

5. MR.: Come on, why won't you marry me today?
   MISS: Oh, I can't make up my mind. I only met you this morning. Don't you think it's a little early?
   MR.: I'm leaving tonight and won't be back for several years. If you don't marry me now, we may never get another chance.

6. "Donate blood today. Due to the recent disaster, thousands are in immediate need of your giving."

7. "Time is running out for you to take advantage of the Carpet Country carpet sale!"

8. "Since these genuine silver spoon sets are intended to be collector's items, they will only be available for a short time."

9. AN ADVERTISEMENT FOR AN ARTHRITIS PAIN RELIEF DRUG FEATURES A PICTURE OF AN ELDERLY LADY EXERCISING IN A PARK: The number one prescription arthritis medicine.

10. "Quick, Pa! The cows are loose, and they're eatin' the neighbor's corn."

11. KID, ATTEMPTING TO GET YOU TO SIGN UP FOR THE NEWSPAPER: I've been delivering this newspaper to your neighbors on both sides for two years.

12. "I'm only going to be in town for a short time, so if you want one, you need to make up your mind soon."

13. "The price of stock in our company has been rising rapidly over the past few weeks, but this won't go on forever; sooner or later the price is going to peak and then drop. You need to buy soon before it reaches its peak."

Lesson 34

Repetition

Someone famous said, "If you can tell a lie long enough and hard enough, sooner or later, people will start believing it."

Repetition is repeating a message loudly and very often in the hope that we will believe it.

"Eat Sugarloops for breakfast! Eat Sugarloops for lunch! Eat Sugarloops for supper! Eat Sugarloops all the time! You will love Sugarloops."

Here, the technique is to drive the thought of eating Sugarloops into our heads – whether or not we would like to eat them at first. The advertiser hopes we will fall under his hypnotic spell and uncontrollably walk over to the cereal aisle of the supermarket mumbling, "Eat Sugarloops…must eat Sugarloops…"

Unlike the example above, sometimes this form of propaganda can't be noticed from only a single quotation. Repetition is also being used when we are bombarded constantly with someone's viewpoint. The person thinks that if he tells his viewpoint often, then people will believe it.

POLITICIAN: I stand in support of hard-working Americans. The kind of American who spends his money on food and health care and doesn't have any left to send his kids through college – I am here to support him. My opponent doesn't share these values. My opponent doesn't care about the hard-working Americans. My opponent does not care about helping the average American put his kids through college. My opponent is all about taking wages from hard-working Americans and giving the money to the rich. Vote for me.

Notice how this politician uses the same phrases over and over?

"Hard-working American" and "my opponent"? This politician does not say how he supports the average American or how his opponent supports the rich – he just keeps using these words over and over in his speeches. He hopes people will eventually believe him – and vote for him.

Calvin uses repetition.

Exercises

A. What form of propaganda, if any, is being used in the following examples?

1. "Try the NEW ABSOLUTELY FREE Car-O-Matic car washer for thirty days. ABSOLUTELY FREE! This item is NEW! If you are not happy with the Car-O-Matic car washer after thirty FREE days, then return it ABSOLUTELY FREE of charge."

2. "No blur. No distortion. Cannon cameras. Share moments. Share life."

3. AN ADVERTISEMENT FOR ALLERGY MEDICINE FEATURES A PICTURE OF MAN WITH A GAS MASK ON: Before nasal allergies change your life, make an easier change. All it takes is Flonase.

4. PICTURE OF YOUNG CHILD SUCKING HER THUMB: Cancer patients aren't the only victims of this disease.

5. "You know what? You are nothing but a stinking bum. You do no work all day, and you sit around doing nothing. I can't believe how lazy you are. You are so lazy that you are going to end up on welfare."

6. "Boy, it seems like everybody's buying one of those balloon gizmos. It must be the latest thing. I think I'll get one."

7. CLYDE: My mom's car can reach very high speeds.
   BERT: How do you know that?
   CLYDE: That's what my mom says, but I don't know how she would know.

8. "Free bagging. Free checking. Free sitting. Free buying. Everything's free at Northpark Mall."

9. MOM: You're not going to wear that, are you?
   DAUGHTER: Aw, Mom. You're so old-fashioned. Everybody's wearing these nowadays.

10. "For ten years I have been telling people that aliens have landed on Earth. Finally, people are beginning to believe me!"

11. LETTER TO PUBLISHER: I am writing to complain about the recent rejection of my book manuscript, *The Fallacy Detective*. I don't think your refusal to publish my book is right. That particular book took me over five years of solid work, without a day of rest. I worked on it so much that the letters on my keyboard are all worn off. I put my whole life into this book, and all you send me is a Post-it note saying, "We are not considering publishing a book on logic at this time." I was heartbroken. It has caused me to lose my sanity.

12. "Clean your house. Clean your car. Clean your garage. Make everything clean with Drakamine."

13. "Ford Explorer."

Lesson 35

Transfer

Transfer is getting us to transfer our good or bad feelings about one thing to another unrelated thing.

Commercials for cleaning products which feature images of spotlessly clean and bright clothes, houses with everything white, and good-looking people are often examples of transfer. The advertiser wants us to transfer our feelings about clean houses and things to their product.

> A handsome man with big, bulging muscles works out on the Gutwrencher exercise machine. He says, "Tone up your muscles in two weeks!"

While this advertiser wouldn't actually say it, he wants us to transfer our feelings about the muscular man to the exercise machine. He wants us to think that if we only bought the exercise machine, then our muscles will start to grow on their own, and, in a few weeks, we will end up looking like the muscular man.

Transfer can also be used to transfer negative feelings.

> Fuzzy images of Candidate B appear. Candidate B is shown on a rainy day wearing a mismatching suit. Discordant music plays in the background. Next, we see a clean image of Candidate A on a clear day in a clean and neat suit. A band plays marching music as a voice says, "Vote for Candidate A. He knows how to govern."

When people see unclear pictures and hear obnoxious music, they start to feel uncomfortable. If the advertiser can make us feel uncomfortable whenever we think about Candidate B, then we will probably feel less inclined to vote for him. If, on the other hand, we see clean images of Candidate A and we hear upbeat inspirational music at the same time, then we might feel more inclined to vote for him when we go to the voting booth.

Transfer is also used when a famous celebrity is used to promote a product.

GARA GORGEOUS, THE FAMOUS MOVIE STAR WITH BEAUTIFUL HAIR, HOLDS UP A BOTTLE OF SHAMPOO: Use Shimmer Bounce shampoo for better-looking and better-smelling hair.

The advertiser wants us to transfer our good feelings for the famous movie star to the shampoo. While Gara Gorgeous's hair was probably done by a professional just before the filming, the advertiser is hoping we will think that her hair looks good because she used Shimmer Bounce shampoo.

Transfer is also used in the naming of products.

"Purefresh Mountain Spring Water"

The name of this product makes us feel like their water is somehow purer and healthier than the everyday kind. They might have gotten it out of the tap, just like everybody else.

Illustration by Rob Corley.

While Porcupine Alarm Systems don't actually use porcupines, the company wants you to transfer your feelings about porcupines to their product.

Not Transfer

Transfer is not being used when the famous person promoting a product is actually an authority on products of that kind.

JACK WACK, THE FAMOUS BASEBALL PITCHER, IS SHOWN HOLDING UP AN ATLANTA SOCKER BASEBALL GLOVE: I always use Atlanta Socker gloves when I pitch. It is the best glove out there.

Jack Wack may have a good reason for using that particular kind of glove – that is, if he actually uses it. We have a reason to believe Atlanta Socker gloves are good.

Exercises

What form of propaganda, if any, is being used in the following examples?

1. JACK WACK, THE FAMOUS BASEBALL PITCHER: I always use Stink-Away deodorant when playing a game – it helps me to smell fresh.

2. JOE BLOWE, THE FAMOUS BOXER: I always exercise with the Gutwrencher exercise machine. I think it helps to build my bulging muscles so I can be a better boxer.

3. "Ladies and gentlemen of the jury, I urge you to convict this man and send him to a place where he can't commit any more crimes. If you don't, you may be his next victim."

4. PICTURE OF A BOTTLE OF SODA POP COVERED IN ICE: Refreshing!

5. PICTURE OF MAN ON TOP OF A VERY TALL TOWER: Car insurance with no State Farm agent? Now that scares me.

6. "Chevy Blazer."

7. AN ADVERTISEMENT FOR CAT FOOD SHOWS A PICTURE OF A HOUSE CAT NEXT TO A LARGE COUGAR: Inside your cat live a thousand generations of big cats. Cats with an insatiable craving for meat. With that in mind, our cat food is made with real chicken.

8. PEOPLE FOR THE ETHICAL TREATMENT OF ANIMALS WEB SITE: Every time you choose to buy a leather jacket or leather shoes, you sentence an animal to a lifetime of suffering.... Fashion should be fun, not grisly!

9. A sport utility vehicle advertisement features an imposing picture of an SUV perched on a rock. Mountains are in the background.

10. "Why can't we go to Disneyland? We probably won't be in California again for several years. This is our only chance."

11. MAN AT THE DOOR: Hello. My name is Scott. I just stopped by to get your opinion on a new encyclopedia. It is very up-to-date and has many different features in it – things such as large sections on each country of the world, with up-to-date information on their geography and current events. In the back, it has poster-size perforated pages of each of the American presidents with statistics on each. I have a plan which you can use to pay for this set over a period of a year. It's up to you.... Boy, it sure is a hot day out today. I was just talking to your neighbors down the road.... Oh, you know them very well? ... Well, I was talking to them, and they couldn't figure out whether they needed this, but after thinking about it, they decided it was important to them.

12. A HAPPY SCENE OF A FATHER WITH A YOUNG SON: I will blink, and he will be grown. At least with my Blue Cross and Blue Shield Plan, I have the power to choose what's right, so I can take charge of his health until he can stand alone. Meanwhile, I will treasure each embrace. This is my plan: to take care of his mind, his body, his spirit, his health.

13. "BFV Motors has now produced over a hundred million cars. A hundred million cars owned by a hundred million drivers."

14. "There's something to be said for the pristine rivers, the breathtaking vistas, the removable third-row seat. Chevy Tahoe. Like a rock."

Lesson 36

Snob Appeal

Snob appeal is the opposite of bandwagon. While bandwagon appeals to our desire to be like everyone else, snob appeal uses our desire to stand out from the rest of the crowd.

Snob appeal is used when someone tries to persuade us to think his product would make us better than or make us stand out from everyone else.

Nobody wants to think he is merely one person among a crowd. We all like to think we're in a small and special community of people – in the uppity -ups.

ADVERTISEMENT: Why read those boring logic books like everybody else does? You know you're better than that. You need more intellectual stimulation. Read *The Fallacy Detective*, and be more logical than the rest.

Snob appeal uses a ridiculous, but very effective line, "Agree with me and buy my product because hardly anybody else does." This is an appeal to our inner snob.

But stop and think for a minute. Maybe there is a good reason why nobody else is doing it.

"Buy Skunk perfume. You will stand out from the crowd."

Military recruiting posters cater to those who want to be "the best of the best."

"Marines. Do you have what it takes?"

Parents who want their children to be distinguished may fall into this trap as well.

"Harrow Boarding School. Improving education for the brightest minds."

The fallacy of snob appeal exploits our desire to be raised up to a higher class. We think that if we purchase the item, then greater glamour and prestige will be given to us. We will become better than everybody else.

Illustration by Rob Corley.

Porcupines: For the discerning pet owner

Exercises

What form of propaganda, if any, is being used?

1. "SPURKEY is a nutritious food. SPURKEY tastes good. Doctors everywhere recommend SPURKEY as a dietary supplement. Remember SPURKEY the next time you go to the grocery store. SPURKEY for America and America for SPURKEY."

2. PICTURE OF AN SUV DRIVING ON ROCKY TERRAIN: It's a rough world. Use the proper equipment.

3. "Envy is so much more pleasant when you're on the receiving end."
   – Mitsubishi car advertisement.

4. "The Smiths are doing it."

5. "We shouldn't proceed with the trial of the senator. The American people are tired and want to get this over with. If you proceed with the trial, then you will be doing something the people do not want."

6. AGRICULTURAL BROCHURE: You don't own a common herd of beef or dairy cattle, so why consider planting a common rye grass pasture? Your cattle investment is best protected by planting Southern Star.

7. A PICTURE OF A PORCUPINE NEXT TO A BOTTLE OF ORANGE JUICE: Our premium orange juice helps support your natural defenses. It only takes a minute, but the feeling lasts all day.

8. "Hey, I hope you agree with us that squealing to the cops isn't the most sociable thing to do. I wouldn't want to lose my best safecracker."

9. AN EYE-POPPINGLY COLORFUL PICTURE OF A FROG: Wildlife as Canon sees it.

10. RATHER EXPENSIVE TOY CATALOGUE: Join Jennifer Lawrence, Josh Hutcherson, and Fred Astaire in owning one of these delightful miniatures.

11. PICTURE OF A FANCY AND FAST-LOOKING SEDAN: Millions of people are perfectly happy driving boring cars. What makes you so special?

12. NISSAN ADVERTISEMENT: May promote feelings of superiority.

13. PICTURE OF PRESIDENTIAL LIMO: On the first day in office, every U.S. president has four things in common with his predecessor. Transporting the Chief on the wings of Goodyear. Goodyear. Specially-designed tires for the leader of the free world.

14. "Florida: America's most popular vacation destination."

15. DEFENSE ATTORNEY: My client admits to committing this crime. However, he has cancer and only a year to live. I think it would be cruel to make a man go to prison when he is in such great pain.

16. "Buy the Chet Atkins Signature Gibson Guitar."

17. "Are you a rising young executive? Our line of luxury hotels caters to people with a taste for the better things in life."

Lesson 37

Appeal to Tradition and Appeal to Hi-Tech

An *appeal to tradition* **occurs when someone encourages us to buy some product or to take some action because it is associated with things of the past.**

This propaganda technique appeals to old-fashioned folk who like old-fashioned traditions.

A BLACK-AND-WHITE PHOTOGRAPH OF MAN BUILDING A GUITAR: Play Martin Guitars. Our expert guitar craftsmen build guitars using only the most time-honored traditions.

Advertising slogans which mention the age of the business are using tradition. "Established in 1919." "We've been in business for over 100 years." They want you to buy because they've been around for a long time. Their age may actually have little to do with their present service.

A VINTAGE BLACK-AND-WHITE PHOTOGRAPH OF A 1950s COUPE ON ONE PAGE, AND ON THE NEXT A NEW PHOTO OF A SMART, MODERN-LOOKING COUPE WHIZZING DOWN THE ROAD: Ford Thunderbird: yesterday, today, and tomorrow.

The first part of this advertisement is an appeal to tradition. It appeals to the sense of stability we get from owning something which has been around for a long time. The second part of the advertisement uses the propaganda technique called *appeal to hi-tech.*

In an *appeal to hi-tech,* we are encouraged to buy something because it is the "latest thing" – not necessarily because it is the best thing.

The picture of the up-to-date car appeals to the good feelings that we may have when we own something which is very new and up-to-date.

> CLYDE: Hey, Bert, you need to buy a pair of these new Niko shoes. They have hi-tech Dinotraction. It's a new special feature which helps you cling onto the back of a running plesiosaur without falling off.

This may be hi-tech, but do I need it? The hi-tech technique is also used when someone uses nonunderstandable technical terms to make his product seem very sophisticated.

> "Our Laundry Ball cleans your clothes automatically with our patented method of defusing the ionization of the fetezoic acids and implanting a catalyst."

Nobody knows what these terms mean, but they sure sound impressive.

Illustration by Rob Corley.

Marge was sold the moment she read "micro-crystals."

Illustration by Rob Corley.

Sometimes people use big words to make themselves sound impressive.

Exercises

What form of propaganda, if any, is being used?

1. PRESIDENT: We need to pass this Nuclear Test Ban Treaty. At any moment, this world could be propelled into a nuclear holocaust.

2. PICTURE OF GEORGE WASHINGTON HOLDING A CAMCORDER: Where the old meets the new. Washington, D.C.

3. "Explosive effects. Dynamic dialogue. Pointed plot. Charismatic characters. This movie is for you."

4. PICTURE OF A CAR BEING DRIVEN IN THE RAIN, PRECARIOUSLY: Treacherous. Could you regain control? Count on Shell.

5. "In order to unlock the secrets of the ocean, Dr. Robert Ballard uses the most sophisticated underwater equipment – including his Rolex Submariner watch."

6. PICTURE OF AN OLD CHEVY SUBURBAN NEXT TO PICTURE OF NEW CHEVY SUBURBAN: Established 1935. Reestablished every year since.

7. "Experience the remarkable attraction of Jenn-Air ovens. For decades, we've been perfecting downdraft ventilation to beautifully clear the air without an overhead hood."

8. "We've been travelin' for several days now, and it seems as if every time we go into a grocery store, gas station, or restaurant, they're playin' country music. I think we're in Texas."

9. "Do you feel as if you are not at your best? Do you feel weak and tired all of the time? Maybe it's because you have parasites living inside you. Parasites are little bugs which live inside you and sap energy from your body. Doctors are beginning to realize that parasites are a leading cause of ill-feeling. Our new patented formula, called 'Bug Away,' helps to remove harmful parasites from your body."

10. "For happier smiles, happier faces, happier families, happier communities, and a happier world. State Ranch Life Insurance."

11. "Café de Columbia coffee. Aromatherapy since 1960."

12. "Visit historic Fredricksport for a touch of the past."

13. "Picked by over one million auto owners as the best sport utility vehicle."

14. PICTURE OF A SMALL, MALNOURISHED, CHILD: Doesn't this poor African child deserve your help?

15. "Stink-Away air freshener. Now with D-432 added for comfort."

16. "But, Dad, this will be my last chance to buy that new dress before they run out."

17. A MAGAZINE ADVERTISEMENT FEATURES A BLACK-AND-WHITE PICTURE OF SOME PEOPLE ROLLING A BARREL OF OLD COUNTRY ROOT BEER ONTO AN OLD PICKUP TRUCK: Some things never change.

18. "The Colorado balrog bush is dying out. We need to halt all logging in the western states until we deal with this problem."

Lesson 38

Find Some Propaganda on Your Own

Exercises

A. Some of the following examples of propaganda use methods not covered in this book. Identify the emotion being appealed to in each.

1. PICTURE OF A YOUNG MAN IN UNIFORM NEXT TO HIS DEVOTED PARENTS: He's not only my son. He's my hero. Today's military. Proud parents. Bright futures.

2. PICTURE OF A PRAIRIE CHICKEN PECKING AT SOME GRASS: The Greater Prairie Chicken is one of several species to benefit from the latest conservation effort by Phillips Petroleum. Together with the National Fish and Wildlife Foundation, Phillips will help restore and manage 19,500 acres of northwestern Missouri, making it a safe haven for high-priority birds. It's just one more way Phillips works to improve our world and why we're known as the Performance Company. Phillips Petroleum Company.

3. "I've just invented a perpetual motion machine which can run your car, power your house, and solve marital disputes all at the same time just

by adding water. Unfortunately, the government wants to cover up my discovery because Exxon and Mobil would lose billions, so now nobody believes me. Just send me $982 plus your firstborn son, and you can have one of my perpetual motion machines."

4. "Oh, a band'll do it, my friends, oh, yes! I mean a boys' band. Do you hear me? I say River City's gotta have a boys' band, and I mean she needs it today. Well, Professor Harold Hill's on hand. River City's gonna have her boys' band! And just as the Lord made little green apples, and that band's gonna be in uniform! Johnny, Willy, Teddy, Fred! And you'll see the glitter of crashing cymbals. And you'll hear the thunder of rolling drums and the shimmer of trumpets. Tah-ta-ra and you'll feel something akin to the electric thrill I once enjoyed when Gilmore, Liberatti, Pat Conway, The Great Creatore, W. C. Handy, and John Philip Sousa all came to town on the very same historic day!" – Professor Harold Hill in *The Music Man*

5. This is the original Kitchener World War I Recruitment poster by Alfred Leete.

6. INSTRUCTIONS TO POLITICAL CANDIDATES: Wear everyday clothes; don't wear anything expensive. If you must dress formal, be plain and simple. In an informal setting, wear jeans. Always make sure your clothes are clean. If you visit a specific group of voters, dress like they're dressed. Wear denim bib overalls and a T-shirt if you're meeting farmers; wear fatigues if you're talking to troops. Use their language too, but don't sound like you're trying to copy their dialect if you can't really pull it off. It might be better to just use a few of their words. Sometimes you can

include a few small errors in your speech to say, "I'm an ordin'ry person. Jus' like you."

7. This is an Australian poster from World War I.

8. ADVERTISEMENT: A vote for John Smith is a vote for Freedom. Our candidate fights for Justice and the Honor of our soldiers. He will stand up for what is Right and Good for Peace in our country.

9. "And so, in the name of all the people who do the work, pay the taxes, raise the kids, and play by the rules, in the name of the hard-working Americans who make up our forgotten middle class, I accept your nomination for President of the United States. I am a product of that middle class. And when I am president, you will be forgotten no

more." – Arkansas Governor Bill Clinton, Democratic National Convention, 1992.

B. 10. Take a current magazine – like *National Geographic*, *Time*, or *Reader's Digest* – and look through all the advertisements in it. Find as many propaganda techniques as you can in the advertisements. You could do the same thing with television commercials.

The Fallacy Detective Game

Illustration by Rob Corley.

Game Rules

In this game, you get to make your own fallacies. We're not trying to learn to recognize fallacies in this game; that's what the rest of this book is for! We invented this game with help from our family and friends.

Preparation

1. Although three players can play this game, it is best played by four or more.
2. Each player must know what a fallacy is and what a propaganda technique is. (You may refer players to the sections of this book that explain fallacies and propaganda techniques.)
   Hint: All of the fallacies covered in this book, with definitions and examples, are listed at the end of these game instructions. You might want to make copies of this list to give to each player.
3. Each player must have paper and a pen or pencil.
4. For beginning players, we recommend that the game be limited to the propaganda techniques in the propaganda section of this book. We think propaganda examples are easier to write and more enjoyable to play with.

Playing the Game

1. All players must create an example of a fallacy or propaganda

technique and write it down – allowing no one else to see what they wrote. Beside their examples, they write the names of the fallacies or propaganda techniques that they have used.

Hint: Creating examples gets easier with each round of the game.

EXAMPLE GAME: Players Bert, Clyde, Jenny, and Sylvia each write down their examples. Bert writes the following example, "A picture of a fur-coat-clad mother hugging young son. Caption reads: 'Feel all warm and fuzzy with our insurance plan.'" Bert also writes what propaganda technique he thinks this is: transfer.

2. One person is chosen to be the first Reader. This person reads the examples from each player, including his own example. He does not say who wrote each example or the names of the fallacies.

EXAMPLE GAME: Jenny is selected as the Reader. She reads the examples from all the players.

3. Each player secretly writes down which example they think was the best. "Best" means whatever each person wants it to mean – funniest, most convincing, or whatever. A player may vote for his own example. The Reader also votes for an example. Each player must *write* his vote down – he cannot *say aloud* which example he is voting for.
4. Each player secretly writes down the name or description of the type of logical fallacy which he has voted for.
5. After everyone has finished writing down their votes, then, beginning with the player to the left of the Reader, each player now says aloud the fallacy he voted for and the name or description of that fallacy.

EXAMPLE GAME: Clyde voted for Bert's example and said it was transfer. Jenny voted for Clyde's example and said it was exigency. Sylvia also voted for Bert's example and said it was snob appeal. Bert voted for Sylvia's example and said it was an appeal to fear. Of course, nobody knew who wrote the example he voted for.

6. The Reader counts the votes and determines which example received the most votes for being "best." If the vote count is tied, then revote.

EXAMPLE GAME: Bert's example is in the majority and is declared the "best."

7. The Reader then determines if the majority votes all agree as to the name of the fallacy they voted for. If some of them disagree, then the Reader determines which fallacy name is in the majority. This fallacy name is assumed to be the correct name of the fallacy in the example. The player who wrote the winning example may have incorrectly named his own example. This does not matter. The majority rules in this game. However, if there is a tie, the person who wrote the example determines what fallacy it is.

EXAMPLE GAME: Since both Clyde and Sylvia voted for Bert's example, his fallacy is declared the "best." But there is a tie. Clyde thinks Bert's example is transfer, while Sylvia thinks Bert's example is snob appeal. Since Bert called it transfer when he created it, what he said is declared the "correct" answer.

Points

1. The player who wrote the best example receives two points.
2. Each player who voted for the best example receives one point.
3. Each player who voted for the best example and who correctly named or described the fallacy or propaganda technique (was in the majority) receives one additional point. Only the Reader does *not* receive a point for guessing correctly the name of the fallacy or propaganda technique he voted for.
4. Points are added up and kept on a separate paper.
5. Note: If the player who wrote the winning fallacy also voted for his own fallacy, then he receives three points. And if he correctly named his own fallacy, he receives four points.

EXAMPLE GAME: Bert receives two points because his fallacy was the "best." Sylvia receives one point because she voted for Bert's example, but she did not correctly identify the fallacy name. Clyde receives two points because he voted for Bert's example and correctly identified the fallacy. Jenny receives no points because she missed all of the above.

Continued Play

1. Play continues with each player writing another fallacy. The next Reader is the player to the right of the previous Reader.
2. The game ends after everyone has had a chance to be the Reader. Or, at the beginning of the game, players may agree to end the game when one player reaches a certain number of points.

Fun We've Had

These are a few examples we came up with while playing this game with friends.

1. TV AD: A child stands wide-eyed as a big truck bears down…darkness…"Let them enjoy life while they can. Juice-Fruit Gum."

2. TV AD: A teddy bear floats face down in water. "Give them a chance to live. Give your children swimming lessons at the Community Y."

3. Lost your reading glasses again? Touch a button and your Spectacle Remote will locate your beeping glasses within a five-mile range!

4. "Ooooh! Aaaah! I feel that warm mud ooze between my toes. Let it all hang out on a vacation to beautiful Maui."

5. A large ugly man mows grass along the roadside. A small green frog sits in the road.
    FROG: Where am I to go?

    A truck comes and smashes the frog. "Let the little creatures live! Don't mow until December."

6. Are you tired of the same old macaroni and cheese? Try our Duke of Windsor Stew. Made in the famous castle by the Duke's own chef many years ago.

7. Buy paper that's inexpensive. Buy paper that's strong. Buy paper that's good. Buy Peter Paper.

8. Are you suffering from fatigue, irritability, or weight gain? Drink Living Well Carrot Juice made from organically grown hand-picked carrots!

9. Visit historic Antarctica: the world's least popular vacation site. Millions of miles of unspoiled wilderness. See dozens of historical explorers frozen in the ice. Don't be the average vacationer.

Short List of Fallacies

These are the fallacies we teach in *The Fallacy Detective*, followed by a few examples.

Avoiding the Question

Red Herring – Introducing an irrelevant point into an argument. Someone may think it proves his side, but it really doesn't.

> LITTLE SISTER: Grizzly bears can't be dangerous – they look so cute.

Special Pleading – Using a double standard or arguing for an unjustified exception.

> GRANDMA: I'm not gambling! This is bingo; not poker. It's different; we're not using a deck of cards.

Ad Hominem – Attacking an opponent's character or his motives for believing something instead of disproving his argument.

> JENNY: My uncle says that all murderers should be put to death because then nobody would want to murder anybody anymore. SYLVIA: Wasn't your uncle in jail once? I don't think that we can trust the opinion of a former criminal.

Genetic Fallacy – Condeming an argument because of where it began, how it began, or who began it.

> BERT: Mr. Gritchus, why do you always wear suspenders and never a belt? MR. GRITCHUS: Because belts were developed in the military centuries ago and were used by soldiers. Since the military is evil, and belts came from the military, therefore I can't wear a belt.

Tu Quoque (You Too) – Dismissing another person's viewpoint on an issue because the speaker is inconsistent in that very thing.

> FRED: I wouldn't smoke cigarettes if I were you. It is a bad habit, and it will bring you all kinds of problems.
> JAKE: Don't tell me not to smoke. You do it too.

Faulty Appeal to Authority – Appealing to the authority of someone who has no special knowledge in the area he is discussing.

> MOTHER: My car mechanic says the best way to fix computer problems is to just give the computer a good, sharp kick.

Appeal to the People – Claiming one's viewpoint is correct just because many other people agree with it.

> POLITICAL CANDIDATE: My opponent thinks this war is killing innocent people despite the fact that a recent poll concluded 76 percent of Americans think it's okay.

Straw Man – Changing or exaggerating an opponent's position to make it easier to refute.

> MRS.: Our car isn't running right. I think we need to buy a better one – something more comfortable.
> MR.: Oh, so you want us to buy a brand new fancy car? I don't think we have enough money for a Rolls Royce.

Making Assumptions

Circular Reasoning – Attempting to prove a conclusion by simply restating it. Someone says "P is true because Q is true, and Q is true because P is true."

JIMMY: Dad, why do I have to learn logic?
DAD: Because it will help to develop your mind.
JIMMY: Why will it develop my mind?
DAD: Because it will help you think better.

Equivocation – Changing the meaning of a word in the middle of an argument.

GRANDMA: If the English don't drive on the right side of the road, what are they doing on the wrong side?

Loaded Question – Asking one question which assumes the answer to a second question.

JUDGE: Have you stopped beating your poor dog yet?

Slippery Slope – Assuming that if we take one step, nothing will stop us from taking a series of steps because each step is the same.

MOTHER: We can't let her get another dog!
FATHER: Oh, we can handle two dogs in the house. She loves animals.
MOTHER: Two dogs? She'll ask for three or four next. This isn't going to stop!

Part-to-Whole – Asserting that what is true of part of something must also be true of the whole thing.

SPORTS REPORTER: Team America was selected from the best players in the United States. Since they are all the best at their positions, this team is going to win.

Whole-to-Part – Asserting that what is true of something as a whole must also be true of each of its parts. This is the reverse of the part-to-whole fallacy.

SPORTS REPORTER: In this year's games, Team America has won more medals than any other team in history. So Jim, who's on Team America, must be a great athlete.

Either-Or – Asserting that we must choose between two things, when in fact we have more than two alternatives.

NEIGHBOR: Either you're an American or you're a Communist. You aren't from America, so you must be a Communist.

Statistical Fallacies

Hasty Generalization – Generalizing about a class based upon a small or poor sample.

HOMEOWNER: All plumbers are brilliant. I know a plumber who can calculate pi to the 289,954th digit.

Weak Analogy – Claiming that some items with only minor similarities are the same in almost everything else.

SCIENTIST: A cloud is 90 percent water. A watermelon is 90 percent water. Since a plane can fly through a cloud. Therefore a plane can fly through a watermelon.

Post Hoc Ergo Propter Hoc – Assuming that since A happened before B, A must have caused B.

FARMER: Our rooster crows every morning. Then the sun comes up. Now do you understand how important roosters are?

Proof by Lack of Evidence – Claiming something is true simply because nobody has yet given any evidence to the contrary.

FARMER: There must be mountain lions living in Illinois because I haven't seen any proof that none exist.

Propaganda

Appeal to Fear – Moving us to fear the consequences of not doing what someone wants.

ADVERTISEMENT: Do you know what kind of damage a loose cow can do on your farm? Imagine what would happen if your electric fence failed and your cows wandered into the neighbor's field. Buy a Zapper electric fence, and you won't have to worry about it.

Appeal to Pity – Urging us to do something only because we pity someone, or we pity something associated with him.

MOTORIST: But officer, this is the fifth ticket I've gotten this year. If I get another ticket, then they will take my license away, and I won't be able to drive to work. My wife and children will starve.

Bandwagon – Pressuring us to do something just because many other people like us are doing it.

CLYDE: Dad, can I go to see the movie *Attack of the Killer Wombats*?
DAD: No, Son, you can't go. I heard that movie has violent scenes in it.
CLYDE: Aw, come on. Everybody's going to see it.

Exigency – Offering nothing more than a time limit as a reason for us to do what someone wants.

ADVERTISEMENT: Genuine lead teacups! Now 95 percent off! Hurry, while supplies last!

Repetition – Repeating a message loudly and very often in the hope that we will believe it.

ADVERTISEMENT: Eat Sugarloops for breakfast! Eat Sugarloops for lunch! Eat Sugarloops for supper! Eat Sugarloops all the time! You will love Sugarloops.

Transfer – Getting us to transfer our good or bad feelings about one thing to another unrelated thing.

GORGEOUS GIRL WITH BEAUTIFUL HAIR HOLDS UP A BOTTLE OF SHAMPOO: Use Shimmer Bounce shampoo for better-looking and better-smelling hair.

Snob Appeal – Encouraging us to think someone's product would make us better than or make us stand out from everybody else.

ADVERTISEMENT: Buy Skunk brand perfume. You will stand out from the crowd.

Appeal to Tradition – Encouraging us to buy a product or do something because it is associated with something old.

BLACK AND WHITE PHOTOGRAPH OF MAN BUILDING A GUITAR: Play Martin Guitars. Our expert guitar craftsmen build guitars using only the most time-honored traditions.

Appeal to Hi-tech – Urging us to buy something because it is the "latest thing" – but not necessarily because it is the best thing.

CLYDE: Hey, Bert, you need to buy a pair of these new Niko shoes. They have hi-tech Dinotraction. It's a new special feature that helps you cling onto the back of a running plesiosaur without falling off.

Answer Key

Illustration by Rob Corley.

Lesson 1: Exercise Your Mind

1. a. Surfing is fun, and maybe valuable, but getting an education is also very valuable. This man seems to be avoiding getting an education.

2. a. Children have the amazing ability to forget things when it suits them. So do adults.

3. c. Ted isn't being lazy with his mind, but he might be lazy with his body.

4. a. Bradley's grandpa is probably trying to get his grandson to think about community issues.

5. b. Mario is making the effort to understand issues better.

6. NATHANIEL: c. Blaine has a point. People with allergies shouldn't have to mow the lawn.
    HANS: c. Blaine is just trying to get out of physical work.

7. b. Kate is probably just complaining. She knows she likes to learn things.

8. c.

Lesson 2: Love to Listen

1. b. Gary doesn't love to listen. He doesn't want to hear people give their side of the issue.

2. c. Can't decide. Betty might just be tired.

3. b. Byron doesn't love to listen. He just made Webster listen to him for half an hour, but he will only listen to Webster for a few seconds.

4. c. Jerry doesn't love to listen to loud music, which is understandable.

5. c. Depends. Generally it's good to listen to criticisms people have for you. But sometimes it can be too much.

6. b. It doesn't sound like Jim is actually worried that Nat is controlling his life. He sounds more like he doesn't want to hear other people criticize his decisions.

7. a. Patty might think she talks too much, but she genuinely wants to listen more.

Lesson 3: Opposing Viewpoints

1. Example: the view of the Union and the view of the Confederacy

2. King George in England's view and the views of the American colonists

3. Raising taxes and lowering taxes

4. Atheists and Christians and Muslims

5. Cubs and White Sox

6. Golden retriever and German shepherd

7. Gun control advocates and Second Amendment rights advocates

8. Creationists and evolutionists

9. Slaveholders in the South and abolitionists in the North

10. Those who read *The Fallacy Detective* and those who don't read *The Fallacy Detective*

11. Mothers and little boys

12. Girls and boys

Lesson 4: Red Herring Fallacy

1. Not a red herring

2. RED HERRING!

3. Not a red herring

4. RED HERRING!

5. RED HERRING!

6. Not a red herring

7. Not a red herring

8. RED HERRING!

Lesson 5: Recognizing Red Herrings

1. Are grizzly bears dangerous? RED HERRING!

2. Should I study math? RED HERRING! This is not the point.

3. Should people read a book a month? Not a red herring.

4. Should the government raise taxes? Not a red herring.

5. Should the government lower taxes? RED HERRING! This shows the government is spending too much money on welfare. It does not show why we should lower taxes. We could eliminate welfare and spend the money somewhere else.

6. Should we believe in life after death? RED HERRING!

7. Would you name as a running mate someone who is against abortion? RED HERRING!

8. Did you ever take drugs? Not a red herring.

9. Did you cheat in school? HANS: I don't think this is a red herring. He doesn't try to avoid the question.

10. Should the federal government help schools? RED HERRING!

11. Is deforestation bad? RED HERRING!

Lesson 6: Special Pleading

1. Red herring

2. Special pleading

3. Special pleading. This is also appeal to pity, which we'll learn about later.

4. Huh?

5. Special pleading

6. Special pleading

7. Probably special pleading

8. Neither. We'll learn about this fallacy soon.

9. Probably special pleading. But, this might be a genuine excuse.

10. Neither

11. Probably special pleading. But, this might be a genuine excuse.

Lesson 7: Ad Hominem Attack

1. *Ad hominem*

2. None

3. *Ad hominem*

4. *Ad hominem*

5. None

6. *Ad hominem*

7. Red herring

8. *Ad hominem*

9. *Ad hominem*

10. Red herring

11. None

12. Special pleading. This army sergeant thinks torturing is okay because his nation is doing it for a good cause. This ignores the question of whether torture is right or wrong – regardless of who is doing it.

13. *Ad hominem*

Lesson 8: Genetic Fallacy

1. None. This is probably true.

2. Genetic fallacy

3. Genetic fallacy

4. Red herring

5. Red herring

6. Genetic fallacy

7. *Ad hominem*

8. None. This is just stating a belief about the origins of fashion.

9. *Ad hominem*

Lesson 9: Tu Quoque

1. *Tu quoque*

2. *Ad hominem*

3. Genetic fallacy

4. None

5. Red herring

6. *Ad hominem*

7. Red herring

8. Red herring. They aren't arguing anymore over whether war is wrong in all cases.

9. *Tu quoque*

10. None. This is merely his opinion.

Lesson 10: Faulty Appeal to Authority

1. Faulty appeal to authority. This man is not an authority on what happened at the scene of the crime.

2. Faulty appeal to authority

3. Good appeal to authority

4. Faulty appeal to authority

5. Good appeal to authority. The violin teacher knows the topic.

6. Faulty appeal to authority

7. Good appeal to authority

8. Good appeal to authority

9. None. Emma Watson is probably an expert on the subject of braces.

10. Red herring. He is changing the subject. They aren't arguing about why he took action. They are arguing about the kind of action he took.

11. Special pleading

12. Faulty appeal to authority

13. None

14. *Ad hominem*

15. Faulty appeal to authority. A high IQ does not make you an expert on movies.

Lesson 11: Appeal to the People

1. Appeal to the people

2. Faulty appeal to authority. This is a controversial topic.

3. Appeal to the people

4. None

5. *Tu quoque*

6. Faulty appeal to authority. This is a very controversial subject.

7. Red herring. It does not say how subsidies will help.

8. Appeal to the people

9. Appeal to the people

10. None. If the song is on the top of the charts, it means many people are listening to it, which means it is popular.

11. *Tu quoque* and appeal to the people

Lesson 12: Straw Man

1. Straw man

2. None. If the book is on the best-seller list, it must be popular.

3. Appeal to the people. Millions of Americans are not authorities on the subject of climate. We need to ask some people who know what they are talking about, and even then we need to examine many different viewpoints about a controversial subject.

4. Appeal to the people

5. Red herring. The question is whether it is morally right to execute insane people, not whether banning the execution of insane people will cause chaos.

6. Straw man. Clyde is not saying that the slaves should not have been freed immediately. He is only saying that it was not the job of the North to invade the South.

7. Appeal to the people

8. Genetic fallacy

9. Straw man

10. Faulty appeal to authority

11. *Tu quoque* and appeal to the people

Lesson 13: The Story of Aroup Goupta

1. True. The story used the masculine pronoun for Aroup.

2. True. Yes, the story said he was in a city.

3. True. The story said he was in a capital city.

4. Don't know. Gotcha. The story mentioned the country called Clovnia, but it did not say if that was where Aroup was.

5. True. It said so.

6. Don't know. The story did not say what Aroup was doing.

7. True. It said so.

8. Don't know. The story never mentioned his age.

9. True. He said that he was Aroup's friend, and we are supposed to believe everything the characters say.

10. True. The story said that it was a restaurant.

11. True. The story said it must have been Cloveneeze.

12. True. You can deduce from the story that he was a native Clovnian.

13. True. He could have been an FBI agent for all we know, but, of course, he could have worked at the restaurant.

14. True. It said so.

15. True. He said that was what he wanted.

16. Don't know. The story never said who they were or why they left the restaurant.

17. True. He said it tasted terrible.

18. True. The story said he felt the oatmeal in his tummy.

19. Don't know. The age limit for drink-ing beet juice was never mentioned.

20. Don't know. She never said she did.

21. Don't know. The story didn't say that Aroup was in trouble.

22. Don't know. The story did end.

Lesson 14: Assumptions

1. Yes

2. Yes

3. No. He said his mom wants to buy an expensive toaster, but he didn't assume all toasters are expensive.

4. Yes. At least the type of ice cream Brent wants.

5. Yes

6. No. This didn't even enter his mind.

7. One. If they sweep them together, then they will have only one pile.

8. The first are worth $19.96, and the second are worth $19.67.

9. If you answered that cows drink milk, then you are wrong. Cows drink water, not milk. A cow would get sick if it drank milk. Notice how we got you to assume something obviously false by subtly suggesting it to your mind.

Lesson 15: Circular Reasoning

1. Circular reasoning

2. Circular reasoning. You can trust him because he says he has never lied? What if he is lying when he says he is not lying?

3. Not circular reasoning

4. Circular reasoning

5. Circular reasoning

6. Not circular reasoning

7. Circular reasoning

8. Not circular reasoning. The hus-band just has a selfish attitude.

9. Not circular reasoning. This is a fallacy that we haven't explained yet.

10. Circular reasoning

11. Circular reasoning

12. Faulty appeal to authority

13. Genetic fallacy

14. Faulty appeal to authority. Gun control is a controversial subject.

15. Yes. Real doctors are those who don't recommend echinacea, and we can know a doctor is real if he doesn't recommend echinacea.

Lesson 16: Equivocation

1. Equivocation on the word "pen"

2. Equivocation on the word "responsible"

3. Equivocation on the word "equal." The founding fathers meant equal under the law, not equal in abilities and incomes.

4. Equivocation on the word "intelligent"

5. None

6. Equivocation on the word "uses"

7. Circular reasoning

8. Equivocation on the word "cold"

9. None

10. None

11. Equivocation on the word "illegal"

12. Faulty appeal to authority

13. Circular reasoning

14. Equivocation on the word "nobody"

Lesson 17: Loaded Question

1. Loaded question. Do you know the music you play can be heard a long distance away? Do you like to disturb the neighborhood?

2. Loaded question. Are you going to buy the Ford Bubblebox model car? If so, when?

3. No loaded question. A mother has the right to ask her children whatever questions she wants.

4. Loaded question. Will the state tourism bureau list our city as smelling bad if we don't ban leaf burning? Should residents be allowed to burn leaves in front of city hall? These controversial questions need to be answered first.

5. Loaded question. Did you know that pain medications are supposed to start to work in one second?

6. Probably a loaded question. Is your business computer in danger of being broken into?

7. Loaded question. Is the president grumpy a lot?

8. Loaded question. The salesperson assumes the lady wants to buy the products.

9. No loaded question

10. Appeal to the people

11. Circular reasoning

12. Probably red herring

13. Equivocation on the word "man"

14. None. Could be true.

15. Special pleading. If humans can't understand psychic languages, how can this actress understand them?

Lesson 18: Slippery Slope

1. Slippery slope

2. Loaded question. Is her husband in a bad mood?

3. Slippery slope

4. This is a proverb, not a fallacy. But this proverb has been used to support slippery slope fallacies.

5. Special pleading

6. NATHANIEL: Slippery slope. The mother should answer her daughter's question, even if she knows her daughter will ask for more later. HANS: Give the poor mom a break. She was right.

7. Huh? None that we can tell.

8. Circular reasoning

9. Special pleading

10. Slippery slope

11. Equivocation on the word "blue"

12. Slippery slope. Clarence Darrow used a slippery slope fallacy to argue for teaching evolution in government schools.

Lesson 19: Part-to-Whole

1. Part-to-whole fallacy

2. Part-to-whole fallacy

3. Not part-to-whole fallacy. We just added those "part… whole" words to confuse you.

4. Part-to-whole fallacy. If the parts of the universe are spherical, then the universe as a whole is spherical.

5. Part-to-whole fallacy. If all the parts of the human body were made for a function, then human beings as a whole also have a purpose.

6. Not part-to-whole fallacy

7. Part-to-whole fallacy. The quality of the materials does not imply that the house was well constructed.

8. Not part-to-whole fallacy

9. Not part-to-whole fallacy. This is actually a fallacy we'll cover in a few lessons. Be patient.

10. Equivocation on the word "crime"

11. Loaded question. Is there evidence for mental telepathy?

12. Circular reasoning

13. Red herring

14. Faulty appeal to authority. Child rearing is a very controversial subject.

15. Huh? None that we can tell.

16. Slippery slope.

17. None. This is a prediction, not a slippery slope fallacy.

Lesson 20: Whole-to-Part

1. Whole-to-part fallacy. Not all of the parts of General Motors cars are made by General Motors.

2. Whole-to-part fallacy. The Smith family as a whole may be a hard-working family, but Bubba Smith may not have those qualities by himself.

3. Whole-to-part fallacy. Even though the farm as a whole may be productive, any particular part of the farm may not be fertile.

4. Part-to-whole fallacy. If each individual is most efficient when he has personal liberty, then society as a whole will reach maximum efficiency if there is maximum personal liberty.

5. None

6. Part-to-whole fallacy. If each American is more aware of danger and is more careful, then all of American society will feel safer.

7. Whole-to-part fallacy. Having a part of a magnificent structure in your home doesn't necessarily make your home any more magnificent.

8. None

9. Loaded question

10. Circular reasoning

11. Whole-to-part fallacy. The fact that the whole economy is booming does not mean that every sector – including the tweezers manufacturing sector – is booming.

12. Equivocation on the word "reason"

13. Appeal to the people

14. Faulty appeal to authority. The First Lady isn't necessarily an expert on this subject.

15. None. The butterfly effect is a scientific theory, not a slippery slope fallacy.

16. Slippery slope

17. Slippery slope

18. Whole-to-part. Harvard may have produced a few bad lawyers over the years.

Lesson 21: Either-Or

1. NATHANIEL: This is either-or. HANS: This is not either-or. It isn't either-or if there are truly only two choices. The farmer is making a good argument that there are only two choices in his experience. Make up your own mind.

2. Either-or

3. Either-or

4. Either-or. The bandit forgot another possibility. "With a heroic bound, Zorro leapt out from the coach and caught the ruffian by the throat…"

5. Not either-or. A mother has the right to limit the alternatives.

6. Either-or

7. Not either-or

8. Not either-or

9. Not either-or. What Dad says goes.

10. Either-or. The neighborhood children could have had a huge squirt gun fight. This is an either-or argument, even though the grumpy old lady considered more than two possibilities.

11. Either-or

12. Either-or

13. Circular reasoning

14. Equivocation on the word "miracles"

15. Appeal to the people

16. Faulty appeal to authority

17. Part-to-whole fallacy. If it is wise for individuals to plan and control their lives, then is it wise for society as a whole to be planned and controlled?

18. Loaded question. Did someone take the fingernail clippers and hide them? If so, who was it?

19. Slippery slope, *tu quoque*, and special pleading

20. None. This is a scientific experiment, not a slippery slope fallacy.

21. Whole-to-part fallacy. Not all Americans share the general characteristics of the American way.

22. Neither. Cows don't drink milk. (Calves do drink milk, but cows do not.) Notice how you were not aware of your assumptions when you

answered that question. Be more alert next time.

Lesson 22: What Is a Generalization?

1. Generalization

2. Generalization

3. Generalization

4. Not a generalization

5. Generalization

6. Not a generalization. There are parts of Alaska on the top of Mt. McKinley, so the statement is true.

7. Not a generalization. If the premises are true, the conclusion must also be true.

8. Generalization

9. Generalization

10. Generalization

11. Not a generalization

12. Generalization

13. Not a generalization

14. Generalization

15. Answers will vary.

Lesson 23: Hasty Generalization

1. Generalization. Sample of one. Very hasty.

2. Generalization. Sample of three thousand. Hasty – probably only rich plumbers would have enough money to attend an international plumbers convention.

3. Generalization. Sample of one. Very hasty – she may teach you well, but there are many different kinds of learners in the world.

4. Not a generalization. "Some" means one or more. Since this man is brilliant (and we must assume he fits whatever he calls "brilliant"), he can accurately say some plumbers are brilliant.

5. Generalization. Sample of all of Dickens's novels. Probably not hasty – but his short stories or letters might be interesting.

6. Generalization. Samples of several times he took aspirin. Strong generalization.

7. Generalization. Sample of five thousand. If the barrel was mixed well, then it is a strong generalization.

8. Not a generalization. The data is complete.

9. Generalization. Sample of one. Very hasty.

10. Probably false. There have been many revolutions where no one was hurt or killed.

11. Answers will vary.

12. Answers will vary. It would be a good idea to study different breeds of pigs in different environments.

13. Answers will vary. You need to see many hairstylists.

14. HANS: I think this is strong. NATHANIEL: I think this is weak. This would take a large sample of firstborns from all over the world.

15. Answers will vary. It would take a large sample of typists in general, and of each person's typing in particular, to decide whether this was a good generalization.

16. You need to survey people in all countries of the world.

17. In our experience: true, except in Florida. It would take a large sample of people in all states south of the Mason-Dixon Line to decide whether this was a good generalization.

18. Answers will vary. A large sample of statistics may indicate this.

19. Probably strong – based on what we know of the Communist governments we can think of.

20. Answers will vary.

Lesson 24: What Is an Analogy?

1. Analogy

2. Generalization

3. Generalization

4. Analogy

5. Analogy

6. Neither

7. Generalization

8. Huh? Neither

9. Neither

10. Analogy – poetic analogy

11. Analogy – poetic analogy

12. Generalization

13. Every time it rains, the flowers will bloom.

14. All southern states that are near the ocean will have palm trees.

15. You will never win a fight against anything that is big and mean like Tony.

Lesson 25: Weak Analogy

1. Weakens

2. Weakens

3. Strengthens

4. It might weaken

5. Weakens

6. Does nothing

7. Strengthens

8. Weakens

9. Strengthens

10. Weakens

11. Weakens

12. Interesting question…
    HANS: I really don't know.

13. Weakens – assuming you are not very young any longer

14. Does nothing

15. Does nothing

16. Weakens

17. HANS: I thought this was a strong analogy, but everybody seems to disagree with me. They all think this is weak. They say the location in the Midwest and near a large body of water has no apparent connection to crime problems.

18. Weak

19. Strong

20. Weak. There is a great difference between one man's life and many, many generations of organisms.

21. Actually, there is much debate over this issue. Some people are afraid of saccharin because of this, and some think that is ridiculous.
    HANS: I say it is probably a weak analogy.

22. Probably strong

23. Neither. This kind of poetic analogy isn't meant to be very scientific but only to illustrate a point.

24. Neither. This kind of poetic analogy isn't meant to be very scientific but only to illustrate a point.

25. Weak

26. Lawyers and mosquitoes

27. It doesn't really. There are some superficial similarities – such as general temperament.

28. That mosquitoes should be able to practice law (if they can pass the bar exam).

29. Answers will vary.

30. Chimpanzees and humans

31. It doesn't really. It doesn't show how animals having some of the same genes and having some of the same social skills as humans makes them significantly similar to humans. It doesn't address the differences between humans and apes at all (such as the amount of hair and the punch bowl).

32. That apes should have some of the same rights as humans.

33. Answers will vary.

Lesson 26: Post Hoc Ergo Propter Hoc

1. Answers will vary. It is also possible that animosity between countries will cause them to build large armies, and if that animosity continues, there may be war.

2. Answers will vary. It might be that I happen to wear those shoes whenever I am in a good mood, and whenever I am in a good mood, I do better on tests.

3. Circular reasoning

4. *Post hoc ergo propter hoc*

5. Whole-to-part fallacy. The power and resources of the United States government as a whole do not necessarily imply that the little mailman at the Wichiwachi Post Office is very powerful or resourceful.

6. Hasty generalization

7. None

8. Weak analogy

9. *Post hoc ergo propter hoc*

10. Either-or

11. Weak analogy

12. Straw man

13. *Post hoc ergo propter hoc*

14. *Post hoc ergo propter hoc*

15. Faulty appeal to authority. Snowboarding versus skiing is a controversial topic. Just because somebody lives in bigger mountains, that doesn't mean they know more about snow sports.

16. None

17. Straw man

18. Slippery slope

19. Equivocation on the word "steal"

Lesson 27: Post Hoc Ergo Propter Hoc in Statistics

1. *Tu quoque*

2. Either-or. He might have been running as an Independent.

3. *Post hoc ergo propter hoc*

4. *Post hoc ergo propter hoc*

5. None. This doesn't say one thing is causing the other.

6. *Post hoc ergo propter hoc*

7. Circular reasoning

8. None. This is not *post hoc ergo propter hoc* because another plausible reason is given for the increase in accidents.

9. None. This is a good appeal to authority.

10. *Post hoc ergo propter hoc*

11. Hasty generalization. He may just become angry at the way you argue with him.

12. Loaded question

13. *Post hoc ergo propter hoc*

14. *Post hoc ergo propter hoc*

15. Special pleading

Lesson 28: Proof by Lack of Evidence

1. Prosecuting Attorney

2. Proof by lack of evidence

3. Weak analogy

4. None

5. Proof by lack of evidence

6. Straw man

7. Whole-to-part. Not all Frenchpeople are sophisticated and artistic.

8. Weak analogy

9. Proof by lack of evidence

10. Either-or

11. Either-or

12. Genetic fallacy

13. Proof by lack of evidence

14. Equivocation on the word "fix"

15. *Post hoc ergo propter hoc*

16. *Ad hominem*

17. Appeal to the people

18. *Post hoc ergo propter hoc*

19. *Post hoc ergo propter hoc*

20. *Post hoc ergo propter hoc*

21. Proof by lack of evidence

22. None

23. None. The researchers don't say that the cabbage is causing auto accidents.

24. Circular reasoning

25. *Ad hominem*

Lesson 29: What Is Propaganda?

1. All kinds: Advertisers, politicians, lawyers, your uncle...

2. No. Good people use propaganda. But good people who are being good shouldn't use manipulative propaganda.

3. Advertisements, political speeches, in the courtroom, from your uncle...

4. No. Propaganda is a general strategy for spreading our ideas. There is nothing wrong with spreading our ideas. But attempting to manipulate people through their emotions is not good.

5. No. They can be correct. Swiss Springtime soap may be good soap, but that doesn't mean the manufacturer should manipulate our emotions.

6. No. When I tell you that Communism is wrong because it destroys society, I am not being manipulative, but I am propagating my beliefs, which is propaganda.

7. No. Propaganda doesn't have to be manipulative, but it often is.

8. No.

9. No

10. Canberra

11. Manipulative

12. Manipulative

13. Manipulative

14. Not manipulative

15. Manipulative

16. Manipulative

Lesson 30: Appeal to Fear

1. Appeal to fear – fear of a car accident

2. Not an appeal to fear

3. Appeal to fear – fear of the consequences if your cows get out

4. Appeal to fear – fear of losing your job

5. Appeal to fear – fear of losing school funding

6. This is a threat, not appeal to fear.

7. Appeal to fear – fear of corrupted kids

8. This is an order, not appeal to fear.

9. This is a threat, not appeal to fear.

10. Appeal to fear – fear of lead poisoning

Lesson 31: Appeal to Pity

1. Appeal to fear

2. Appeal to pity. It doesn't say how controlling guns would solve the problem.

3. None – yet.

4. Appeal to pity.
   TEACHER: You should have thought about that when you were studying for the test.

5. Appeal to pity. He doesn't say that he actually needs any money.

6. None – assuming that he is telling the truth, the guy obviously needs help.

7. Appeal to fear – fear of fire

8. Appeal to pity

9. None – yet.

10. Appeal to pity

11. None

12. Appeal to both fear and pity

Lesson 32: Bandwagon

1. Appeal to pity

2. Bandwagon

3. Bandwagon

4. Appeal to fear

5. Appeal to pity

6. Bandwagon

7. Bandwagon

8. None

9. Bandwagon

10. None – yet.

Lesson 33: Exigency

1. Exigency. But do I want one?

2. Bandwagon

3. Exigency. What if I don't want a new house?

4. Bandwagon

5. Exigency. He gives no real reason to marry him.

6. None. It gives a good reason to give blood today: many people need it.

7. Exigency

8. Exigency

9. Bandwagon

10. None

11. Bandwagon

12. Exigency

13. None. If you really want to make money, you need to buy now. We could call this a legitimate exigency.

Lesson 34: Repetition

1. Repetition
2. Repetition
3. Appeal to fear and exigency
4. Appeal to pity and fear
5. Repetition
6. Bandwagon
7. None
8. Repetition
9. Bandwagon
10. Repetition
11. Appeal to pity
12. Repetition
13. None – yet.

Lesson 35: Transfer

1. Transfer. Jack Wack has no special expertise in this subject.
2. None
3. Appeal to fear – the fear of becoming a victim.
4. Transfer
5. Appeal to fear
6. Transfer. The "Blazer" prompts us to think that the owner will automatically become a rugged individualist.

7. Transfer. Will our cat become a mountain lion if it eats their cat food?
8. Appeal to pity
9. Transfer
10. Exigency
11. Bandwagon
12. Transfer
13. Bandwagon
14. Transfer

Lesson 36: Snob Appeal

1. Repetition
2. Transfer
3. Snob appeal
4. Bandwagon
5. Bandwagon
6. Snob appeal
7. Transfer
8. Appeal to fear
9. Transfer. They want you to think that if you owned a Canon camera, then you would be able to take pictures like the one shown.
10. Snob appeal
11. Snob appeal
12. Snob appeal
13. Transfer and snob appeal

14. Bandwagon

15. Appeal to pity

16. Snob appeal and transfer

17. Snob appeal

Lesson 37: Appeal to Tradition and Appeal to Hi-Tech

1. Exigency and appeal to fear

2. Transfer, appeal to tradition, and appeal to hi-tech

3. Transfer and repetition

4. Appeal to fear

5. Appeal to hi-tech

6. Appeal to tradition

7. Appeal to tradition and hi-tech

8. None

9. Appeal to fear and hi-tech

10. Repetition

11. Appeal to tradition

12. Appeal to tradition

13. Bandwagon

14. Appeal to pity

15. Appeal to hi-tech

16. Exigency

17. Appeal to tradition

18. Exigency

Lesson 38: Find Some Propaganda on Your Own

1. This appeals to American patriotism and pride.

2. Phillips wants us to support their company because they care about the environment. We don't know if they make these efforts because they really care about the environment or because they just want to be able to post advertisements like this.

3. This is similar to snob appeal. Some people want to believe they have the "inside track" on information which no one else has. Sometimes it feels good to think we are a small, repressed group, struggling to get our message out.

4. Professor Harold Hill is a good crowd stirrer. He uses the kind of language which sways large groups of people – mobs. He uses many different propaganda techniques. We could call his general method of manipulation *mob appeal*.

5. This appeals to British patriotism and pride.

6. This appeals to "plain folks" or our desire to be like everybody else.

7. This is just an ordinary appeal to fear.

8. This uses words like "freedom" and "justice" and "God" to make us feel good.

9. This appeals to our desire to have a
    candidate who is like us. This is like
    the "plain folks" appeal.

10. Answers will vary.

Made in the USA
San Bernardino, CA
08 July 2019